THE LIFE OF
HENRY THE FIFTH

EDITED BY

ROBERT D. FRENCH

LVX ET VERITAS

NEW HAVEN · YALE UNIVERSITY PRESS
LONDON : GEOFFREY CUMBERLEGE
OXFORD UNIVERSITY PRESS

Copyright, 1918
By Yale University Press
Printed in the United States of America

First published, September, 1918
Second printing, March, 1931
Third printing, June, 1944
Fourth printing, December, 1946
Fifth printing, August, 1948
Sixth printing, September, 1953

TABLE OF CONTENTS

*The facsimile opposite represents the title-page of the Eliza-
bethan Club copy of the first edition of 'Henry V.' Five other
copies are known. It is remarkable that none of the three
quarto editions of this play bear the author's name.*

THE
CRONICLE
History of Henry the fift,

With his battell fought at *Agin Court* in
France. Togither with *Auntient*
Pistoll.

As it hath bene sundry times playd by the Right honorable
the Lord Chamberlaine his seruants.

LONDON

Printed by *Thomas Creede,* for Tho. Milling-
ton, and Iohn Busby. And are to be
sold at his house in Carter Lane, next
the Powle head. 1600.

[DRAMATIS PERSONÆ

KING HENRY THE FIFTH
DUKE OF GLOUCESTER,
DUKE OF BEDFORD, } *Brothers to the King*
DUKE OF CLARENCE,
DUKE OF EXETER, *Uncle to the King*
DUKE OF YORK, *Cousin to the King*
EARLS OF SALISBURY, WESTMORELAND, and WARWICK
ARCHBISHOP OF CANTERBURY
BISHOP OF ELY
EARL OF CAMBRIDGE
LORD SCROOP OF MASHAM
SIR THOMAS GREY
SIR THOMAS ERPINGHAM, GOWER, FLUELLEN, MACMORRIS, JAMY, *Officers in King Henry's Army*
BATES, COURT, WILLIAMS, *Soldiers in the Same*
PISTOL, NYM, BARDOLPH
Boy
A Herald

CHARLES THE SIXTH, *King of France*
LEWIS, *the Dauphin*
DUKES OF BURGUNDY, ORLEANS, and BOURBON
The CONSTABLE OF FRANCE
RAMBURES and GRANDPRÉ, *French Lords*
MONTJOY, *a French Herald*
Governor of Harfleur
Ambassadors to the King of England
ISABEL, *Queen of France*
KATHARINE, *Daughter to Charles and Isabel*
ALICE, *a Lady attending on the Princess Katharine*
Hostess of the Boar's Head Tavern, *formerly Mistress Quickly, and now married to Pistol*
Lords, Ladies, Officers, French and English Soldiers, Citizens, Messengers, and Attendants

Chorus

SCENE: *England to the close of Act II. Sc. iii;
afterwards France*]

S. shows Hen. V as an ideal King.
Play re monarchy, leadership, what a
king should do. Greatest "war" play.
More powerful, profound, less partial then modern
plays & novels:

The Life of Henry the Fifth

Enter Prologue.

O! for a Muse of fire, that would ascend
The brightest heaven of invention;
A kingdom for a stage, princes to act
And monarchs to behold the swelling scene.　　4
Then should the warlike Harry, like himself,
Assume the port of Mars; and at his heels,
Leash'd in like hounds, should famine, sword, and fire
Crouch for employment. But pardon, gentles all,
The flat unraised spirits that hath dar'd　　9
On this unworthy scaffold to bring forth
So great an object: can this cockpit hold
The vasty fields of France? or may we cram　　12
Within this _wooden O_ the very casques
That did affright the air at Agincourt?
O, pardon! since a crooked figure may
Attest in little place a million;　　16
And let us, ciphers to this great accompt,
On your imaginary forces work.
Suppose within the girdle of these walls
Are now confin'd two mighty monarchies,　　20
Whose high upreared and abutting fronts
The perilous narrow ocean parts asunder:
Piece out our imperfections with your thoughts:
Into a thousand parts divide one man,　　24
And make imaginary puissance;
Think when we talk of horses that you see them

Explains in-
adequacy of
stage to justify
action,
begs the
audience
to lend their
imagination
to enjoy this
play. He asks
for spacial
& temporal
compression

6 port: *bearing*　　9 unraised: *unaspiring*　　10 scaffold: *stage*
11 cockpit; *cf. n.*　　　　　　　　　　　　　　　12 vasty: *vast*
13 the very casques: *even the helmets*　　16 Attest: *stand for; cf. n.*
17 accompt: *account*　　　　　　　　18 imaginary: *imaginative*
21 abutting: *adjacent*

Printing their proud hoofs i' the receiving earth;
For 'tis your thoughts that now must deck our
    kings,   28
Carry them here and there, jumping o'er times,
Turning the accomplishment of many years
Into an hour-glass: for the which supply,
Admit me Chorus to this history;   32
Who prologue-like your humble patience pray,
Gently to hear, kindly to judge, our play.   *Exit.*

*[handwritten: very static, great amt of dialogue
S. teaches Eliz-
ethans (in pit) history to clarify Hen's
claim to Franc]*

ACT FIRST

Scene One

[*London. An Antechamber in the King's Palace*]

Enter the two Bishops of Canterbury and Ely

    Cant. My lord, I'll tell you; that self bill is urg'd,
Which in th' eleventh year of the last king's reign
Was like, and had indeed against us pass'd,
But that the scambling and unquiet time   4
Did push it out of further question.

    Ely. But how, my lord, shall we resist it now?

    Cant. It must be thought on.   If it pass against us,
We lose the better half of our possession;   8
For all the temporal lands which men devout
By testament have given to the church
Would they strip from us; being valu'd thus:
As much as would maintain, to the king's honour,   12
Full fifteen earls and fifteen hundred knights,
Six thousand and two hundred good esquires;

29 jumping o'er times; *cf. n.*
31 for . . . supply: *for which service*   32 Chorus; *cf. n.*
Scene One S. d. Bishops; *cf. n.*   1 self: *same*   3 like: *likely (to pass)*
4 scambling: *turbulent*   5 question: *consideration*

And, to relief of lazars and weak age,
Of indigent faint souls past corporal toil,   16
A hundred almshouses right well supplied;
And to the coffers of the king beside,
A thousand pounds by the year.   Thus runs the bill.
    Ely.   This would drink deep.
    Cant.   'Twould drink the cup and all.
    Ely. But what prevention?   21
    Cant. The king is full of grace and fair regard.
    Ely. And a true lover of the holy church.
    Cant. The courses of his youth promis'd it not.   24
The breath no sooner left his father's body
But that his wildness, mortified in him,
Seem'd to die too; yea, at that very moment,
Consideration like an angel came,   28
And whipp'd the offending Adam out of him,
Leaving his body as a paradise,
To envelop and contain celestial spirits.
Never was such a sudden scholar made;   32
Never came reformation in a flood,
With such a heady currance, scouring faults;
Nor never Hydra-headed wilfulness
So soon did lose his seat and all at once   36
As in this king.
    Ely.   We are blessed in the change.
    Cant. Hear him but reason in divinity,
And, all-admiring, with an inward wish
You would desire the king were made a prelate: 40
Hear him debate of commonwealth affairs,
You would say it hath been all in all his study:
List his discourse of war, and you shall hear

---

15 lazars: *beggars (especially lepers)*   26 mortified: *subdued*
28 Consideration: *reflection*   34 heady currance: *headlong current*
35 Hydra-headed: *many-headed; cf. n.*   36 his: *its*
43 List: *listen to*

A fearful battle render'd you in music: 44
Turn him to any cause of policy,
The Gordian knot of it he will unloose,
Familiar as his garter; that, when he speaks,
The air, a charter'd libertine, is still,   48
And the mute wonder lurketh in men's ears,
To steal his sweet and honey'd sentences;
So that the art and practic part of life
Must be the mistress to this theoric: 52
Which is a wonder how his Grace should glean it,
Since his addiction was to courses vain;
His companies unletter'd, rude, and shallow;
His hours fill'd up with riots, banquets, sports;   56
And never noted in him any study,
Any retirement, any sequestration
From open haunts and popularity.

    Ely. The strawberry grows underneath the nettle,
And wholesome berries thrive and ripen best   61
Neighbour'd by fruit of baser quality:
And so the prince obscur'd his contemplation
Under the veil of wildness; which, no doubt,   64
Grew like the summer grass, fastest by night,
Unseen, yet crescive in his faculty.

    Cant. It must be so; for miracles are ceas'd;
And therefore we must needs admit the means
How things are perfected.

    Ely.   But, my good lord,   69
How now for mitigation of this bill
Urg'd by the commons? Doth his majesty
Incline to it, or no?

---

45 cause of policy: *political question*   46 Gordian knot; *cf. n.*
47 that: *so that*   48 charter'd: *privileged*
51 art; *cf. n.*   practic: *practical*   52 theoric: *theory*
55 companies: *companions*   57 never noted: *there was never noted*
58 sequestration: *withdrawal*   59 popularity: *low company*
63 contemplation: *thoughtful nature*
66 crescive in his faculty: *increasing by its own power*

Cant.   He seems indifferent,   72
Or rather swaying more upon our part
Than cherishing the exhibiters against us;
For I have made an offer to his majesty,
Upon our spiritual convocation,   76
And in regard of causes now in hand,
Which I have open'd to his Grace at large,
As touching France, to give a greater sum
Than ever at one time the clergy yet   80
Did to his predecessors part withal.
  Ely. How did this offer seem receiv'd, my lord?
  Cant. With good acceptance of his majesty;
Save that there was not time enough to hear,—   84
As I perceiv'd his Grace would fain have done,—
The severals and unhidden passages
Of his true titles to some certain dukedoms,
And generally to the crown and seat of France,
Deriv'd from Edward, his great-grandfather.   89
  Ely. What was the impediment that broke this off?
  Cant. The French ambassador upon that instant
Crav'd audience; and the hour I think is come
To give him hearing: is it four o'clock?   93
  Ely. It is.
  Cant. Then go we in to know his embassy;
Which I could with a ready guess declare   96
Before the Frenchman speak a word of it.
  Ely. I'll wait upon you, and I long to hear it.
                                              Exeunt.

73 upon our part: *to our side*
74 exhibiters: *i.e., those who presented the bill in Parliament*
76 Upon: *upon the authority of*   81 withal: *with*
86 severals: *details*   passages: *lines of succession*
89 Edward; *cf. n.*   95 embassy: *message*

great change of Prince Hal.

Scene Two

[The Presence Chamber]

Enter the King, Humphrey [Duke of Gloucester],
Bedford, Clarence, Warwick, Westmoreland, and
Exeter [with Attendants].

K. Hen. Where is my gracious lord of Canterbury?
Exe. Not here in presence.
K. Hen.   Send for him, good uncle.
West. Shall we call in the ambassador, my liege?
K. Hen. Not yet, my cousin: we would be re-
    solv'd,   4
Before we hear him, of some things of weight
That task our thoughts, concerning us and France.

Enter [the] two Bishops.

Cant. God and his angels guard your sacred throne,
And make you long become it!
K. Hen.   Sure, we thank you.
My learned lord, we pray you to proceed,   9
And justly and religiously unfold
Why the law Salique that they have in France
Or should, or should not, bar us in our claim.   12
And God forbid, my dear and faithful lord,
That you should fashion, wrest, or bow your reading,
Or nicely charge your understanding soul
With opening titles miscreate, whose right   16
Suits not in native colours with the truth;
For God doth know how many now in health
Shall drop their blood in approbation

---

4 cousin: *title of courtesy used by the sovereign in addressing a*
  nobleman   4, 5 resolv'd . . . of: *satisfied about*   6 task: *trouble*
8 become: *grace*   11 law Salique: *Salic law; cf. n.*   12 Or: *either*
14 wrest: *pervert*   15 nicely: *sophistically*   charge: *burden*
16 opening: *disclosing*   miscreate: *dishonestly invented*
19 approbation: *proof*

humane monarch—
shows great humility.

Of what your reverence shall incite us to.   20
Therefore take heed how you impawn our person,
How you awake our sleeping sword of war:
We charge you in the name of God, take heed;
For never two such kingdoms did contend   24
Without much fall of blood; whose guiltless drops
Are every one a woe, a sore complaint,
'Gainst him whose wrongs give edge unto the swords
That make such waste in brief mortality.   28
Under this conjuration speak, my lord,
For we will hear, note, and believe in heart,
That what you speak is in your conscience wash'd
As pure as sin with baptism.   32
    Cant. Then hear me, gracious sovereign, and you
       peers,
That owe yourselves, your lives, and services
To this imperial throne.   There is no bar
To make against your highness' claim to France   36
But this, which they produce from Pharamond,
In terram Salicam mulieres ne succedant,
'No woman shall succeed in Salique land':
Which Salique land the French unjustly gloze   40
To be the realm of France, and Pharamond
The founder of this law and female bar.
Yet their own authors faithfully affirm
That the land Salique is in Germany,   44
Between the floods of Sala and of Elbe;
Where Charles the Great, having subdu'd the Saxons,
There left behind and settled certain French;
Who, holding in disdain the German women   48
For some dishonest manners of their life,

[intro.
to "war"
theme
& the
ideal
king.]

---

21 impawn: *pledge*   28 mortality: *human life*
37 Pharamond: *legendary Frankish king*   40 gloze: *interpret*
45 floods: *rivers*   46 Charles the Great: *Charlemagne*
49 dishonest: *unchaste*

Establish'd then this law; to wit, no female
Should be inheritrix in Salique land:
Which Salique, as I said, 'twixt Elbe and Sala,
Is at this day in Germany call'd Meisen.   53
Then doth it well appear the Salique law
Was not devised for the realm of France;
Nor did the French possess the Salique land   56
Until four hundred one-and-twenty years
After defunction of King Pharamond,
Idly suppos'd the founder of this law;
Who died within the year of our redemption   60
Four hundred twenty-six; and Charles the Great
Subdu'd the Saxons, and did seat the French
Beyond the river Sala, in the year
Eight hundred five. Besides, their writers say,
King Pepin, which deposed Childeric,   65
Did, as heir general, being descended
Of Blithild, which was daughter to King Clothair,
Make claim and title to the crown of France.   68
Hugh Capet also, who usurp'd the crown
Of Charles the Duke of Lorraine, sole heir male
Of the true line and stock of Charles the Great,
To find his title with some shows of truth,—   72
Though in pure truth, it was corrupt and naught,—
Convey'd himself as th' heir to the Lady Lingare,
Daughter to Charlemain, who was the son
To Lewis the emperor, and Lewis the son   76
Of Charles the Great. Also King Lewis the Tenth,
Who was sole heir to the usurper Capet,
Could not keep quiet in his conscience,
Wearing the crown of France, till satisfied   80

57 Cf. n.   58 defunction: *death*   65 King Pepin; *cf. n.*
69 Hugh Capet; *cf. n.*   72 find: *provide*
74 Convey'd himself: *passed himself off*
75 Charlemain: *i.e., Charles the Bald*   77 Lewis the Tenth; *cf. n.*

That fair Queen Isabel, his grandmother,
Was lineal of the Lady Ermengare,
Daughter to Charles the aforesaid Duke of Lorraine:
By the which marriage the line of Charles the
    Great   84
Was re-united to the crown of France.
So that, as clear as is the summer's sun,
King Pepin's title, and Hugh Capet's claim,
King Lewis his satisfaction, all appear   88
To hold in right and title of the female:
So do the kings of France unto this day;
Howbeit they would hold up this Salique law
To bar your highness claiming from the female;
And rather choose to hide them in a net   93
Than amply to imbar their crooked titles
Usurp'd from you and your progenitors.
    K. Hen. May I with right and conscience make this
      claim?   96
    Cant. The sin upon my head, dread sovereign!
For in the book of Numbers is it writ:
'When the man dies, let the inheritance
Descend unto the daughter.' Gracious lord,   100
Stand for your own; unwind your bloody flag;
Look back into your mighty ancestors:
Go, my dread lord, to your great-grandsire's tomb,
From whom you claim; invoke his warlike spirit,   104
And your great-uncle's, Edward the Black Prince,
Who on the French ground play'd a tragedy,
Making defeat on the full power of France;
Whiles his most mighty father on a hill   108
Stood smiling to behold his lion's whelp
Forage in blood of French nobility.

82 lineal: *direct descendant*   88 King Lewis his: *King Lewis'*
93 them: *themselves*   94 *Cf. n.*
98 Numbers; *cf. Numb. 27. 8.*   106-114 *Cf. n.*

O noble English! that could entertain
With half their forces the full pride of France,
And let another half stand laughing by,   113
All out of work, and cold for action.

 Ely. Awake remembrance of these valiant dead,
And with your puissant arm renew their feats:
You are their heir, you sit upon their throne,
The blood and courage that renowned them
Runs in your veins; and my thrice-puissant liege
Is in the very May-morn of his youth,   120
Ripe for exploits and mighty enterprises.

 Exe. Your brother kings and monarchs of the earth
Do all expect that you should rouse yourself,
As did the former lions of your blood.   124

 West. They know your Grace hath cause and means
  and might;
So hath your highness; never King of England
Had nobles richer, and more loyal subjects,
Whose hearts have left their bodies here in Eng-
  land   128
And lie pavilion'd in the fields of France.

 Cant. O! let their bodies follow, my dear liege,
With blood and sword and fire to win your right;
In aid whereof we of the spiritualty   132
Will raise your highness such a mighty sum
As never did the clergy at one time
Bring in to any of your ancestors.

 K. Hen. We must not only arm to invade the
  French,   136
But lay down our proportions to defend
Against the Scot, who will make road upon us

114 for: *for want of*   116 puissant: *powerful*
120 May-morn of his youth; *cf. n.*
126 So hath your highness; *cf. n.*   132 spiritualty: *clergy*
137 lay . . . proportions: *estimate the requisite number of troops*
138 road: *inroad*

With all advantages.

    Cant. They of those marches, gracious sover-
      eign,   140
Shall be a wall sufficient to defend
Our inland from the pilfering borderers.

    K. Hen. We do not mean the coursing snatchers
      only,
But fear the main intendment of the Scot,   144
Who hath been still a giddy neighbour to us;
For you shall read that my great-grandfather
Never went with his forces into France
But that the Scot on his unfurnish'd kingdom
Came pouring, like the tide into a breach,   149
With ample and brim fulness of his force,
Galling the gleaned land with hot assays,
Girding with grievous siege castles and towns;
That England, being empty of defence,   153
Hath shook and trembled at the ill neighbourhood.

    Cant. She hath been then more fear'd than harm'd,
      my liege;
For hear her but exampled by herself: 156
When all her chivalry hath been in France
And she a mourning widow of her nobles,
She hath herself not only well defended,
But taken and impounded as a stray   160
The King of Scots; whom she did send to France,
To fill King Edward's fame with prisoner kings,
And make your chronicle as rich with praise
As is the ooze and bottom of the sea   164
With sunken wrack and sumless treasuries.

    West. But there's a saying very old and true;

---

140 marches: *borders*   143 coursing snatchers: *marauding pilferers*
144 intendment: *intention*   145 still: *always*   giddy: *unstable*
148 unfurnish'd: *undefended*   151 assays: *attacks*
155 fear'd: *frightened*   160 impounded: *imprisoned; cf. n.*
165 wrack: *wreckage*

'If that you will France win,
          Then with Scotland first begin':   168
For once the eagle England being in prey,
To her unguarded nest the weasel Scot
Comes sneaking and so sucks her princely eggs,
Playing the mouse in absence of the cat,   172
To tear and havoc more than she can eat.
     Exe. It follows then the cat must stay at home:
Yet that is but a crush'd necessity;
Since we have locks to safeguard necessaries   176
And pretty traps to catch the petty thieves.
While that the armed hand doth fight abroad,
The advised head defends itself at home:
For government, though high and low and lower,   180
Put into parts, doth keep in one consent,
Congreeing in a full and natural close,
Like music.
     Cant.   Therefore doth heaven divide
The state of man in divers functions,   184
Setting endeavour in continual motion;
To which is fixed, as an aim or butt,
Obedience: for so work the honey-bees,
Creatures that by a rule in nature teach   188
The act of order to a peopled kingdom.
They have a king and officers of sorts;
Where*some, like magistrates, correct at home,
Others, like merchants, venture trade abroad,   192
Others, like soldiers, armed in their stings,
Make boot upon the summer's velvet buds;
Which pillage they* with merry march bring home
To the tent-royal of their emperor: 196

---

169 in prey: *in search of prey*   175 crush'd: *forced*
181 parts: *used in the musical sense*   consent: *harmony*
182 Congreeing: *agreeing*   close: *cadence*
190 sorts: *different ranks*   194 Make boot upon: *plunder*

Who, busied in his majesty, surveys
The singing masons building roofs of gold,
The civil citizens kneading up the honey,
The poor mechanic porters crowding in   200
Their heavy burdens at his narrow gate,
The sad-ey'd justice, with his surly hum,
Delivering o'er to executors pale
The lazy yawning drone. I this infer,   204
That many things, having full reference
To one consent, may work contrariously;
As many arrows, loosed several ways,
Come to one mark; as many ways meet in one
          town;   208
As many fresh streams meet in one salt sea;
As many lines close in the dial's centre;
So may a thousand actions, once afoot,
End in one purpose, and be all well borne   212
Without defeat. Therefore to France, my liege.
Divide your happy England into four;
Whereof take you one quarter into France,
And you withal shall make all Gallia shake.   216
If we, with thrice such powers left at home,
Cannot defend our own doors from the dog,
Let us be worried and our nation lose
The name of hardiness and policy.   220
    K. Hen. Call in the messengers sent from the
       Dauphin.   [*Exit an Attendant.*]
Now are we well resolv'd; and by God's help,
And yours, the noble sinews of our power,
France being ours, we'll bend it to our awe   224
Or break it all to pieces: or there we'll sit,
Ruling in large and ample empery

only ¼
will go to
France, ¾
will defend
the borders

199 civil: *civilian*   202 sad-ey'd: *sober-looking*
203 executors: *executioners*   216 withal: *therewith*
220 policy: *political wisdom*   226 empery: *empire*

O'er France and all her almost kingly dukedoms,
Or lay these bones in an unworthy urn,   228
Tombless, with no remembrance over them:
Either our history shall with full mouth
Speak freely of our acts, or else our grave,
Like   Turkish   mute,   shall   have   a   tongueless
      mouth,   232
Not worshipp'd with a waxen epitaph.

Enter Ambassadors of France.

Now are we well prepar'd to know the pleasure
Of our fair cousin Dauphin; for we hear
Your greeting is from him, not from the king.
      First Amb. May 't please your majesty to give us
            leave   237
Freely to render what we have in charge;
Or shall we sparingly show you far off
The Dauphin's meaning and our embassy?   240
      K. Hen. We are no tyrant, but a Christian king;
Unto whose grace our passion is as subject
As are our wretches fetter'd in our prisons:
Therefore   with   frank   and   with   uncurbed   plain-
      ness   244
Tell us the Dauphin's mind.
      First Amb.   Thus then, in few.
Your highness, lately sending into France,
Did claim some certain dukedoms, in the right
Of   your   great   predecessor,   King   Edward   the
      Third.   248
In answer of which claim, the prince our master
Says that you savour too much of your youth,
And bids you be advis'd there's nought in France

231 freely: *generously*
233 worshipp'd: *honored*   waxen: *perishable*
245 in few: *briefly*   251 be advis'd: *consider*

That can be with a nimble galliard won;   252
You cannot revel into dukedoms there.
He therefore sends you, meeter for your spirit,
This tun of treasure; and, in lieu of this,
Desires you let the dukedoms that you claim   256
Hear no more of you.   This the Dauphin speaks.
   K. Hen. What treasure, uncle?
   Exc.   Tennis-balls, my liege.
   K. Hen. We are glad the Dauphin is so pleasant
     with us:
His present and your pains we thank you for:
When we have match'd our rackets to these balls,   261
We will in France, by God's grace, play a set
Shall strike his father's crown into the hazard.
Tell him he hath made a match with such a
     wrangler   264
That all the courts of France will be disturb'd
With chaces.   And we understand him well,
How he comes o'er us with our wilder days,
Not measuring what use we made of them.   268
We never valu'd this poor seat of England;
And therefore, living hence, did give ourself
To barbarous licence; as 'tis ever common
That men are merriest when they are from home.   272
But tell the Dauphin I will keep my state,
Be like a king and show my sail of greatness
When I do rouse me in my throne of France:
For that I have laid by my majesty   276
And plodded like a man for working-days,
But I will rise there with so full a glory
That I will dazzle all the eyes of France,

252 galliard: *a lively dance*   254 meeter: *more fitting*
255 tun: *a cask*   in lieu of: *in return for*
259 pleasant: *facetious*   263 hazard: *part of a tennis-court*
266 chaces; *cf. n.*   267 comes o'er: *taunts*
269 seat: *throne*   270 living hence; *cf. n.*

Yea, strike the Dauphin blind to look on us.   280
And tell the pleasant prince this mock of his
Hath turn'd his balls to gun-stones; and his soul
Shall stand sore-charged for the wasteful vengeance
That shall fly with them: for many a thousand
        widows   284
Shall this his mock mock out of their dear husbands;
Mock mothers from their sons, mock castles down;
And some are yet ungotten and unborn
That shall have cause to curse the Dauphin's
        scorn.   288
But this lies all within the will of God,
To whom I do appeal; and in whose name
Tell you the Dauphin I am coming on,
To venge me as I may and to put forth   292
My rightful hand in a well-hallow'd cause.
So get you hence in peace; and tell the Dauphin
His jest will savour but of shallow wit
When thousands weep more than did laugh at it.   296
Convey them with safe conduct.   Fare you well.
                                    Exeunt Ambassadors.
  Exe. This was a merry message.
  K. Hen. We hope to make the sender blush at it.
Therefore, my lords, omit no happy hour   300
That may give furtherance to our expedition;
For we have now no thought in us but France,
Save those to God, that run before our business.
Therefore let our proportions for these wars   304
Be soon collected, and all things thought upon
That may with reasonable swiftness add
More feathers to our wings; for, God before,   307
We'll chide this Dauphin at his father's door.

282 gun-stones: *cannon balls (originally made of stone)*
287 ungotten: *not begotten*   304 proportions: *levies*
307 God before: *with God's help*

Therefore let every man now task his thought,
That this fair action may on foot be brought.

                Exeunt.

ACT SECOND

Flourish. Enter Chorus.

Now all the youth of England are on fire,
And silken dalliance in the wardrobe lies;
Now thrive the armourers, and honour's thought
Reigns solely in the breast of every man: 4
They sell the pasture now to buy the horse,
Following the mirror of all Christian kings,
With winged heels, as English Mercuries.
For now sits Expectation in the air   8
And hides a sword from hilts unto the point
With crowns imperial, crowns and coronets,
Promis'd to Harry and his followers.
The French, advis'd by good intelligence   12
Of this most dreadful preparation,
Shake in their fear, and with pale policy
Seek to divert the English purposes.
O England! model to thy inward greatness,   16
Like little body with a mighty heart,
What mightst thou do, that honour would thee do,
Were all thy children kind and natural!
But see thy fault! France hath in thee found out   20
A nest of hollow bosoms, which he fills
With treacherous crowns; and three corrupted men,
One, Richard Earl of Cambridge, and the second,

Act Second S. d. Flourish: *music of trumpets*
12 intelligence: *reconnaissance*   14 policy: *trickery*
18 would: *would have*   19 kind: *true to their kinship*
20 France: *the king of France*   22 crowns: *crown-pieces, gold*

Henry Lord Scroop of Masham, and the third,
Sir Thomas Grey, knight, of Northumberland,
Have, for the gilt of France,—O guilt, indeed!—
Confirm'd conspiracy with fearful France;
And by their hands this grace of kings must die,— 28
If hell and treason hold their promises,—
Ere he take ship for France, and in Southampton.
Linger your patience on, and we'll digest
The abuse of distance; force a play.   32
The sum is paid; the traitors are agreed;
The king is set from London; and the scene
Is now transported, gentles, to Southampton:
There is the playhouse now, there must you sit:
And thence to France shall we convey you safe,
And bring you back, charming the narrow seas
To give you gentle pass; for, if we may,
We'll not offend one stomach with our play.   40
But, till the king come forth and not till then,
Unto Southampton do we shift our scene.   *Exit.*

. Comic subplot intro, in II
instead of I in
Hen. IV, ,2.

Scene One

[*London. A street*]

Enter Corporal Nym and Lieutenant Bardolph.

Bard. Well met, Corporal Nym.

Nym. Good morrow, Lieutenant Bardolph.

Bard. What, are Ancient Pistol and you
friends yet?   4

Nym. For my part, I care not: I say little;
but when time shall serve, there shall be smiles;

26 gilt: *gold*
28 grace of kings: *he who does honor to the title of king*
31, 32 *Cf. n.*   34 is set: *has set out*
41, 42 *Cf. n.*   3 Ancient: *Ensign*   39 pass: *passage*
                                                      6 smiles; *cf. n.*

but that shall be as it may. I dare not fight;
but I will wink and hold out mine iron. It is a
simple one; but what though? it will toast
cheese, and it will endure cold as another man's
sword will: and there's an end.   11

Bard. I will bestow a breakfast to make you
friends, and we'll be all three sworn brothers to
France: let it be so, good Corporal Nym.

Nym. Faith, I will live so long as I may,
that's the certain of it; and when I cannot live
any longer, I will do as I may: that is my rest,
that is the rendezvous of it.   18

Bard. It is certain, corporal, that he is
married to Nell Quickly; and, certainly she did
you wrong, for you were troth-plight to her.   21

Nym. I cannot tell; things must be as they
may: men may sleep, and they may have their
throats about them at that time; and, some say,
knives have edges. It must be as it may: though
patience be a tired mare, yet she will plod.
There must be conclusions. Well, I cannot tell.

Enter Pistol and [Hostess] Quickly.

Bard. Here comes Ancient Pistol and his
wife. Good corporal, be patient here. How
now, mine host Pistol!

Pist. Base tike, call'st thou me host?
Now, by this hand, I swear, I scorn the term;   32
Nor shall my Nell keep lodgers.

Host. No, by my troth, not long; for we cannot lodge and board a dozen or fourteen gentle-
women that live honestly by the prick of their

---

8 wink: *shut my eyes*   11 there's an end: *cf. n.*
17 rest: *resolve; cf. n.*   18 rendezvous; *cf. n.*
21 troth-plight: *betrothed*   31 tike: *cur*

needles, but it will be thought we keep a bawdy-
house straight. O well-a-day, Lady! if
he be not drawn now: we shall see wilful
adultery and murder committed.   40

Bard. Good lieutenant! good corporal! offer
nothing here.

Nym. Pish!

Pist. Pish for thee, Iceland dog! thou prick-ear'd
cur of Iceland!   44

Host. Good Corporal Nym, show thy valour
and put up your sword.

Nym. Will you shog off? I would have you
solus.

Pist. Solus, egregious dog? O viper vile!
The *solus* in thy most mervailous face;
The *solus* in thy teeth, and in thy throat,
And in thy hateful lungs, yea, in thy maw, perdy;
And, which is worse, within thy nasty mouth!   53
I do retort the *solus* in thy bowels;
For I can take, and Pistol's cock is up,
And flashing fire will follow.   56

Nym. I am not Barbason; you cannot conjure me. I have an humour to knock you in-
differently well. If you grow foul with me, Pistol,
I will scour you with my rapier, as I may, in
fair terms: if you would walk off, I would prick
your guts a little, in good terms, as I may; and
that's the humour of it.

Pist. O braggart vile and damned furious
wight!   64
The grave doth gape, and doting death is near;
Therefore exhale.

38 Lady: *an oath by the Virgin Mary*   44 Iceland dog; *cf. n.*
47 shog: *move*   50 mervailous: *marvelous*   52 perdy: *par Dieu*
55 take: *take fire*   57 Barbason: *name of a fiend; cf. n.*
66 exhale: *draw forth (thy sword)*

Bard. Hear me, hear me what I say: he that
strikes the first stroke, I'll run him up to the
hilts, as I am a soldier.   [*Draws.*]

Pist. An oath of mickle might, and fury shall abate.
Give me thy fist, thy fore-foot to me give;
Thy spirits are most tall.   72

Nym. I will cut thy throat, one time or other,
in fair terms; that is the humour of it.

Pist. 'Couple a gorge!'
That is the word.   I thee defy again.   76
O hound of Crete, think'st thou my spouse to get?
No; to the spital go,
And from the powdering-tub of infamy
Fetch forth the lazar kite of Cressid's kind,   80
Doll Tearsheet she by name, and her espouse:
I have, and I will hold, the quondam Quickly
For the only she; and—pauca, there's enough.
Go to.

                    Enter the Boy.

Boy. Mine host Pistol, you must come to my
master, and your hostess: he is very sick, and
would to bed.   Good Bardolph, put thy face between his sheets and do the office of a warming-
pan.   Faith, he's very ill.   88

Bard. Away, you rogue!

Host. By my troth, he'll yield the crow a
pudding one of these days.   The king has killed
his heart.   Good husband, come home presently.
                          Exit [with Boy].

Bard. Come, shall I make you two friends?

70 mickle might: *great weight*   72 tall: *valiant*
75 Couple a gorge: *coupe la gorge*   77 hound of Crete; *cf. n.*
78 spital: *hospital*   79 powdering-tub; *cf. n.*
80 the lazar kite of Cressid's kind; *cf. n*   83 pauca: *briefly*
86 thy face; *cf. n.*   92 presently: *immediately*

We must to France together. Why the devil
should we keep knives to cut one another's
throats?   96

Pist. Let floods o'erswell, and fiends for food
  howl on!

   Nym. You'll pay me the eight shillings I won
of you at betting?

Pist. Base is the slave that pays.   100

   Nym. That now I will have; that's the
humour of it.

Pist. As manhood shall compound: push home.

                                        Draw.

   Bard. By this sword, he that makes the first
thrust, I'll kill him; by this sword, I will.   105

Pist. Sword is an oath, and oaths must have their
  course.

   Bard. Corporal Nym, an thou wilt be friends,
be friends: an thou wilt not, why then, be enemies with me too. Prithee, put up.   109

   Nym. I shall have my eight shillings I won
of you at betting?

Pist. A noble shalt thou have, and present pay;
And liquor likewise will I give to thee,   113
And friendship shall combine, and brotherhood:
I'll live by Nym, and Nym shall live by me.
Is not this just? for I shall sutler be   116
Unto the camp, and profits will accrue.
Give me thy hand.

   Nym. I shall have my noble?

Pist. In cash most justly paid.

   Nym. Well then, that's the humour of it.   121

---

103 compound: *decide*   107 an: *if*
112 noble: *6s. 8d.*
116 sutler: *one who sells provisions and liquor*

Enter Hostess.

Host. As ever you came of women, come in
quickly to Sir John. Ah, poor heart! he is so
shaked of a burning quotidian tertian, that it is
most lamentable to behold. Sweet men, come to
him.

Nym. The king hath run bad humours on
the knight; that's the even of it.   128

Pist. Nym, thou hast spoke the right;
His heart is fracted and corroborate.

Nym. The king is a good king: but it must
be as it may; he passes some humours and
careers.   133

Pist. Let us condole the knight; for, lambkins, we
will live.   [*Exeunt.*]

Scene Two

[*Southampton.   A Council-chamber*]

Enter Exeter, Bedford, and Westmoreland.

Bed. 'Fore God, his Grace is bold to trust these
traitors.

Exe. They shall be apprehended by and by.

West. How smooth and even they do bear themselves!

As if allegiance in their bosoms sat,   4

Crowned with faith and constant loyalty.

Bed. The king hath note of all that they intend,

By interception which they dream not of.

Exe. Nay, but the man that was his bedfellow,

124 quotidian tertian; *cf. n.*
128 the even of it; *cf.* 'the long and the short of it'
130 fracted: *broken*   corroborate; *cf. n.*
133 careers; *cf. n.*   134 condole: *sympathize with*
2 by and by: *immediately*

Whom he hath dull'd and cloy'd with gracious
    favours,   8
That he should, for a foreign purse, so sell
His sovereign's life to death and treachery!

Sound trumpets. Enter the King, Scroop, Cambridge,
        and Grey [with Attendants].

  K. Hen. Now sits the wind fair, and we will
    aboard.   12
My Lord of Cambridge, and my kind Lord of
    Masham,
And you, my gentle knight, give me your thoughts:
Think you not that the powers we bear with us
Will cut their passage through the force of
    France,   16
Doing the execution and the act
For which we have in head assembled them?
  Scroop. No doubt, my liege, if each man do his
    best.
  K. Hen. I doubt not that; since we are well per-
    suaded   20
We carry not a heart with us from hence
That grows not in a fair consent with ours;
Nor leave not one behind that doth not wish
Success and conquest to attend on us.   24
  Cam. Never was monarch better fear'd and lov'd
Than is your majesty: there's not, I think, a subject
That sits in heart-grief and uneasiness
Under the sweet shade of your government.   28
  Grey. True: those that were your father's enemies
Have steep'd their galls in honey, and do serve you
With hearts create of duty and of zeal.
  K. Hen. We therefore have great cause of thank-
    fulness,   32

15 powers: *forces*   18 in head: *as an army*

And shall forget the office of our hand,
Sooner than quittance of desert and merit
According to the weight and worthiness.

    Scroop. So service shall with steeled sinews
      toil,   36
And labour shall refresh itself with hope,
To do your Grace incessant services.

    K. Hen. We judge no less. Uncle of Exeter,
Enlarge the man committed yesterday   40
That rail'd against our person: we consider
It was excess of wine that set him on;
And on his more advice we pardon him.

    Scroop. That's mercy, but too much security:
Let him be punish'd, sovereign, lest example   45
Breed, by his sufferance, more of such a kind.

    K. Hen. O! let us yet be merciful.

    Cam. So may your highness, and yet punish too. 48

    Grey. Sir,
You show great mercy, if you give him life
After the taste of much correction.

    K. Hen. Alas! your too much love and care of
      me   52
Are heavy orisons 'gainst this poor wretch.
If little faults, proceeding on distemper,
Shall not be wink'd at, how shall we stretch our eye
When capital crimes, chew'd, swallow'd, and di-
      gested,   50
Appear before us? We'll yet enlarge that man,
Though Cambridge, Scroop, and Grey, in their dear
      care,
And tender preservation of our person,

34 quittance: *reward*   40 Enlarge: *set free*
43 his more advice: *his return to greater coolness of mind*
46 by his sufferance: *because he is pardoned*
53 orisons: *petitions*
54 proceeding on distemper: *arising from drunkenness*

Would have him punish'd. And now to our French
    causes: 60
Who are the late commissioners?
   Cam. I one, my lord:
Your highness bade me ask for it to-day.
   Scroop. So did you me, my liege.   64
   Grey. And I, my royal sovereign.
   K. Hen. Then, Richard, Earl of Cambridge, there
    is yours;
There yours, Lord Scroop of Masham; and, sir knight,
Grey of Northumberland, this same is yours: 68
Read them; and know, I know your worthiness.
My Lord of Westmoreland, and uncle Exeter,
We will aboard to-night. Why, how now, gentlemen!
What see you in those papers that you lose   72
So much complexion? Look ye, how they change!
Their cheeks are paper. Why, what read you there,
That hath so cowarded and chas'd your blood
Out of appearance?
   Cam.   I do confess my fault,   76
And do submit me to your highness' mercy.
   Grey.   ⎫
   Scroop. ⎬ To which we all appeal.
   K. Hen. The mercy that was quick in us but late
By your own counsel is suppress'd and kill'd: 80
You must not dare, for shame, to talk of mercy;
For your own reasons turn into your bosoms,
As dogs upon their masters, worrying you.
See you, my princes and my noble peers,   84
These English monsters! My Lord of Cambridge
   here,
You know how apt our love was to accord

puts Eng.
as su-
preme
value,
lies on-
ly one
course
in
treason

61 the late commissioners: *those lately commissioned*
63 it: *i.e., his commission*   79 quick: *alive*
86 apt: *ready*   accord: *consent*

To furnish him with all appertinents
Belonging to his honour; and this man   88
Hath, for a few light crowns, lightly conspir'd,
And sworn unto the practices of France,
To kill us here in Hampton: to the which
This knight, no less for bounty bound to us   92
Than Cambridge is, hath likewise sworn. But O!
What shall I say to thee, Lord Scroop? thou cruel,
Ingrateful, savage and inhuman creature!
Thou that didst bear the key of all my counsels,
That knew'st the very bottom of my soul,   97
That almost mightst have coin'd me into gold
Wouldst thou have practis'd on me for thy use!
May it be possible that foreign hire   100
Could out of thee extract one spark of evil
That might annoy my finger? 'tis so strange
That, though the truth of it stands off as gross
As black and white, my eye will scarcely see it.
Treason and murder ever kept together,   105
As two yoke-devils sworn to either's purpose,
Working so grossly in a natural cause
That admiration did not whoop at them: 108
But thou, 'gainst all proportion, didst bring in
Wonder to wait on treason and on murder:
And whatsoever cunning fiend it was
That wrought upon thee so preposterously   112
Hath got the voice in hell for excellence:
And other devils that suggest by treasons
Do botch and bungle up damnation
With patches, colours, and with forms, being
          fetch'd   116

90 unto the practices: *in accord with the plots*
91 Hampton: *Southampton*
108 admiration: *wonder*
112 preposterously: *contrary to the natural order of things*
113 voice: *verdict*
107 grossly: *palpably*
109 proportion: *seemliness*
114 suggest: *seduce*

From glistering semblances of piety;
But he that temper'd thee bade thee stand up,
Gave thee no instance why thou shouldst do treason,
Unless to dub thee with the name of traitor.   120
If that same demon that hath gull'd thee thus
Should with his lion gait walk the whole world,
He might return to vasty Tartar back,
And tell the legions, 'I can never win   124
A soul so easy as that Englishman's.'
O! how hast thou with jealousy infected
The sweetness of affiance. Show men dutiful?
Why, so didst thou: seem they grave and learned?   128
Why, so didst thou: come they of noble family?
Why, so didst thou: seem they religious?
Why, so didst thou: or are they spare in diet,
Free from gross passion or of mirth or anger,   132
Constant in spirit, not swerving with the blood,
Garnish'd and deck'd in modest complement,
Not working with the eye without the ear,
And but in purged judgment trusting neither?   136
Such and so finely bolted didst thou seem:
And thus thy fall hath left a kind of blot,
To mark the full-fraught man and best indu'd
With some suspicion. I will weep for thee;   140
For this revolt of thine, methinks, is like
Another fall of man. Their faults are open:
Arrest them to the answer of the law;
And God acquit them of their practices!   144

117 glistering: *glittering*
118 temper'd: *moulded (to his purpose)*   stand up; *cf. n.*
119 instance: *motive*   123 Tartar: *Tartarus (the classical hell)*
126 jealousy: *suspicion*   127 affiance: *trust*   Show: *appear*
133 blood: *passion*   134 complement: *external appearance*
136 but in purged judgment: *except after careful scrutiny*
137 bolted: *sifted; i.e., tested*
139 full-fraught: *fully laden (with virtues)*   best indu'd: *most richly endowed*

Exe. I arrest thee of high treason, by the
name of Richard Earl of Cambridge.

I arrest thee of high treason, by the name of
Henry Lord Scroop of Masham.   148

I arrest thee of high treason, by the name of
Thomas Grey, knight, of Northumberland.

Scroop. Our purposes God justly hath discover'd,
And I repent my fault more than my death;   152
Which I beseech your highness to forgive,
Although my body pay the price of it.

Cam. For me, the gold of France did not seduce,
Although I did admit it as a motive   156
The sooner to effect what I intended:
But God be thanked for prevention;
Which I in sufferance heartily will rejoice,
Beseeching God and you to pardon me.   160

Grey. Never did faithful subject more rejoice
At the discovery of most dangerous treason
Than I do at this hour joy o'er myself,
Prevented from a damned enterprise.   164
My fault, but not my body, pardon, sovereign.

K. Hen. God quit you in his mercy! Hear your
  sentence.
You have conspir'd against our royal person,
Join'd with an enemy proclaim'd, and from his
  coffers   168
Receiv'd the golden earnest of our death;
Wherein you would have sold your king to slaughter,
His princes and his peers to servitude,
His subjects to oppression and contempt,   172
And his whole kingdom into desolation.
Touching our person seek we no revenge;

151 discover'd: *revealed*   155-157 *Cf. n.*
159 in sufferance: *while suffering the penalty*
166 quit: *pardon*   169 earnest: *pledge money*

But we our kingdom's safety must so tender,
Whose ruin you have sought, that to her laws   176
We do deliver you.   Get you therefore hence,
Poor miserable wretches, to your death;
The taste whereof, God of his mercy give
You patience to endure, and true repentance   180
Of all your dear offences! Bear them hence.
  Exeunt [*Cambridge, Scroop, and Grey, guarded*].
Now, lords, for France! the enterprise whereof
Shall be to you, as us, like glorious.
We doubt not of a fair and lucky war,   184
Since God so graciously hath brought to light
This dangerous treason lurking in our way
To hinder our beginnings.   We doubt not now
But every rub is smoothed on our way.   188
Then forth, dear countrymen: let us deliver
Our puissance into the hand of God,
Putting it straight in expedition.
Cheerly to sea! the signs of war advance: 192
No king of England, if not king of France.
     Flourish.   [*Exeunt.*]

brilliant mixture of comedy &
pathos.

Scene Three

[*London.   A street*]

Enter Pistol, Nym, Bardolph, Boy, and Hostess.

 Host. Prithee, honey-sweet husband, let me
bring thee to Staines.
 Pist. No; for my manly heart doth yearn.

175 tender: *cherish*   181 dear: *grievous*
183 like: *in equal degree*   188 rub: *obstacle*
191 straight: *at once* expedition: *motion*
192 signs: *standards* advance: *raise*
2 bring: *accompany* Staines: *first stage on the road from London to*
 Southampton   3 yearn: *grieve*

Bardolph, be blithe; Nym, rouse thy vaunting
    veins;   4
Boy, bristle thy courage up; for Falstaff he is dead,
And we must yearn therefore.

    Bard. Would I were with him, wheresome'er
he is, either in heaven or in hell!   8

    Host. Nay, sure, he's not in hell: he's in Ar-
thur's bosom, if ever man went to Arthur's bosom. A' made a finer end and went away an it
had been any christom child; a' parted even just 12
between twelve and one, even at the turning o'
the tide: for after I saw him fumble with the
sheets and play with flowers and smile upon his
fingers' ends, I knew there was but one way; for 16
his nose was as sharp as a pen, and a' babbled of
green fields. 'How now, Sir John!' quoth I:
'what, man! be of good cheer.' So a' cried out
'God, God, God!' three or four times: now I, 20
to comfort him, bid him a' should not think of
God, I hoped there was no need to trouble himself with any such thoughts yet. So a' bade me
lay more clothes on his feet: I put my hand 24
into the bed and felt them, and they were as
cold as any stone; then I felt to his knees, and
so upward, and upward, and all was as cold as
any stone.   28

    Nym. They say he cried out of sack.

    Host. Ay, that a' did.

    Bard. And of women.

    Host. Nay, that a' did not.   32

---

9 Arthur's bosom; *cf. n.*   11 A': *he*   an: *as if*
12 christom: *not yet a month old*
17, 18 and a' babbled of green fields; *cf. n.*
29 of: *against*   sack: *a white wine*

Boy. Yes, that a' did; and said they were devils incarnate.

Host. A' could never abide carnation; 'twas a colour he never liked.   36

Boy. A' said once, the devil would have him about women.

Host. A' did in some sort, indeed, handle women; but then he was rheumatic, and talked of the whore of Babylon.   41

Boy. Do you not remember a' saw a flea stick upon Bardolph's nose, and a' said it was a black soul burning in hell-fire?   44

Bard. Well, the fuel is gone that maintained that fire: that's all the riches I got in his service.

Nym. Shall we shog? the king will be gone from Southampton.   49

Pist. Come, let's away. My love, give me thy lips.
Look to my chattels and my moveables:
Let senses rule, the word is, 'Pitch and pay';   52
Trust none;
For oaths are straws, men's faiths are wafer-cakes,
And hold-fast is the only dog, my duck:
Therefore, *'caveto'* be thy counsellor.   56
Go, clear thy crystals. Yoke-fellows in arms,
Let us to France; like horse-leeches, my boys,
To suck, to suck, the very blood to suck!

Boy. And that's but unwholesome food, they say.   61

Pist. Touch her soft mouth, and march.
Bard. Farewell, hostess.   [*Kissing her.*]

39 handle: *talk of*   40 rheumatic: *error for 'lunatic'*
52 senses: *prudence*   word: *motto*   Pitch and pay: *cash down*
54 wafer-cakes: *i.e., very fragile*   56 caveto: *beware*
57 clear thy crystals: *dry your eyes* (*?*)

Nym. I cannot kiss, that is the humour of
it; but, adieu.   65

Pist. Let housewifery appear: keep close, I
thee command.

Host. Farewell; adieu.   *Exeunt.*

*handles the French
brilliantly.*

*over-civilized
over-confident
shrewd
not cowards*

Scene Four

[*France.   An Apartment in the French King's
Palace*]

*Flourish.   Enter the French King, the Dauphin, the
Dukes of Berri and Bretagne [the Constable,
and Others].*

Fr. King. Thus comes the English with full power
upon us;

And more than carefully it us concerns

*a bit whacky
effeminate*

To answer royally in our defences.

Therefore the Dukes of Berri and Bretagne,   4

Of Brabant and of Orleans, shall make forth,

And you, Prince Dauphin, with all swift dispatch,

To line and new repair our towns of war

With men of courage and with means defendant: 8

For England his approaches makes as fierce

As waters to the sucking of a gulf:

It fits us then to be as provident

As fear may teach us, out of late examples   12

Left by the fatal and neglected English

Upon our fields.

Dau.   My most redoubted father,

It is most meet we arm us 'gainst the foe;

---

66 housewifery: *economy*   Scene Four S. d. Constable; *cf. n.*
2 more than carefully: *with more than common care*
7 line: *strengthen*   9 England: *the king of England*
10 gulf: *whirlpool*   13 fatal and neglected: *fatally neglected*

*presents French in this way for the
moment of the Elizabethans.*

For peace itself should not so dull a kingdom,—
Though war nor no known quarrel were in ques-
    tion,—   17
But that defences, musters, preparations,
Should be maintain'd, assembled, and collected,
As were a war in expectation.   20
Therefore, I say 'tis meet we all go forth
To view the sick and feeble parts of France:
And let us do it with no show of fear;
No, with no more than if we heard that England
Were busied with a Whitsun morris-dance: 25
For, my good liege, she is so idly king'd,
Her sceptre so fantastically borne
By a vain, giddy, shallow, humorous youth,   28
That fear attends her not.

    Con.   O peace, Prince Dauphin!
You are too much mistaken in this king.
Question your Grace the late ambassadors,
With what great state he heard their embassy,
How well supplied with noble counsellors,   33
How modest in exception, and withal
How terrible in constant resolution,
And you shall find his vanities forespent   36
Were but the outside of the Roman Brutus,
Covering discretion with a coat of folly;
As gardeners do with ordure hide those roots
That shall first spring and be most delicate.   40

    Dau. Well, 'tis not so, my lord high constable;
But though we think it so, it is no matter:
In cases of defence 'tis best to weigh
The enemy more mighty than he seems: 44
So the proportions of defence are fill'd;

[margin note: hitting at Hen's youth.]

25 Whitsun morris-dance; *cf. n.*   28 humorous: *full of whims*
34 exception: *offering objections*
36 forespent: *past*   37 Brutus; *cf. n.*

[handwritten note: Fr. believe English are crude.]

Which of a weak and niggardly projection
Doth like a miser spoil his coat with scanting
A little cloth.

    Fr. King. Think we King Harry strong;   48
And, princes, look you strongly arm to meet him.
The kindred of him hath been flesh'd upon us,
And he is bred out of that bloody strain
That haunted us in our familiar paths: 52
Witness our too much memorable shame
When Cressy battle fatally was struck
And all our princes captiv'd by the hand
Of that black name, Edward Black Prince of
    Wales;   56
Whiles that his mountain sire, on mountain standing,
Up in the air, crown'd with the golden sun,
Saw his heroical seed, and smil'd to see him
Mangle the work of nature, and deface   60
The patterns that by God and by French fathers
Had twenty years been made. This is a stem
Of that victorious stock; and let us fear
The native mightiness and fate of him.   64

            Enter a Messenger.

    Mess. Ambassadors from Harry King of England
Do crave admittance to your majesty.
    Fr. King. We'll give them present audience. Go,
and bring them.
        [Exeunt Messenger and certain Lords.]
You see this chase is hotly follow'd, friends.   68
    Dau. Turn head, and stop pursuit; for coward dogs
Most spend their mouths when what they seem to
    threaten

---

46 projection: *calculation*   50 been flesh'd: *preyed; cf. n.*
57 mountain sire: *mighty father*
64 fate: *what he is destined to perform*   67 present: *immediate*

Runs far before them. Good my sovereign,
Take up the English short, and let them know
Of what a monarchy you are the head: 73
Self-love, my liege, is not so vile a sin
As self-neglecting.

Enter Exeter [with Lords and train].

  Fr. King.   From our brother of England?
  Exe. From him; and thus he greets your maj-
      esty.   76
He wills you, in the name of God Almighty,
That you divest yourself, and lay apart
The borrow'd glories that by gift of heaven,
By law of nature and of nations 'long   80
To him and to his heirs; namely, the crown
And all wide-stretched honours that pertain
By custom and the ordinance of times
Unto the crown of France. That you may know
'Tis no sinister nor no awkward claim,   85
Pick'd from the worm-holes of long-vanish'd days,
Nor from the dust of old oblivion rak'd,
He sends you this most memorable line,   88
In every branch truly demonstrative;
Willing you overlook this pedigree;
And when you find him evenly deriv'd
From his most fam'd of famous ancestors,   92
Edward the Third, he bids you then resign
Your crown and kingdom, indirectly held
From him the native and true challenger.
  Fr. King. Or else what follows?   96
  Exe. Bloody constraint: for if you hide the crown
Even in your hearts, there will he rake for it:

---

80 'long: *belong*   85 sinister: *unfair*   awkward: *perverse*
88 line: *pedigree*   91 evenly deriv'd: *directly descended*
94 indirectly: *wrongfully*

Therefore in fierce tempest is he coming,　　　*compares*
In thunder and in earthquake like a Jove,　　100　*Hen. to a*
That, if requiring fail, he will compel;　←　*God,*
And bids you, in the bowels of the Lord,
Deliver up the crown, and to take mercy　　　*starts*
On the poor souls for whom this hungry war　104　*the Fr.*
Opens his vasty jaws; and on your head　　　*thinking*
Turning the widows' tears, the orphans' cries,
The dead men's blood, the pining maidens' groans,
For husbands, fathers, and betrothed lovers,　108
That shall be swallow'd in this controversy.
This is his claim, his threat'ning, and my message;
Unless the Dauphin be in presence here,
To whom expressly I bring greeting too.　　112
　　Fr. King. For us, we will consider of this further:
To-morrow shall you bear our full intent
Back to our brother of England.
　　Dau.　　　　　　　　For the Dauphin,
I stand here for him: what to him from Eng-
　　land?　　　　　　　　　　　　　116
　　Exe. Scorn and defiance, slight regard, contempt,
And anything that may not misbecome
The mighty sender, doth he prize you at.
Thus says my king: an if your father's highness　120
Do not, in grant of all demands at large,
Sweeten the bitter mock you sent his majesty,
He'll call you to so hot an answer of it,
That caves and womby vaultages of France　124
Shall chide your trespass and return your mock
In second accent of his ordnance.
　　Dau. Say, if my father render fair return,
It is against my will; for I desire　　　　128

101 requiring: *requesting*　　　　102 in the bowels: *by the mercy*
124 womby vaultages: *deep caverns*
126 second accent of his ordnance: *echoes of his cannon*

Nothing but odds with England: to that end,
As matching to his youth and vanity,
I did present him with the Paris balls.

    Exe. He'll make your Paris Louvre shake for
      it,   132
Were it the mistress-court of mighty Europe:
And, be assur'd, you'll find a difference—
As we his subjects have in wonder found—
Between the promise of his greener days   136
And these he masters now.   Now he weighs time
Even to the utmost grain; that you shall read
In your own losses, if he stay in France.

    Fr. King. To-morrow shall you know our mind at
      full.   *Flourish.*   140

    Exe. Dispatch us with all speed, lest that our king
Come here himself to question our delay;
For he is footed in this land already.

    Fr. King. You shall be soon dispatch'd with fair
      conditions: 144
A night is but small breath and little pause
To answer matters of this consequence.   *Exeunt.*

ACT THIRD

Flourish.   Enter Chorus.

Thus with imagin'd wing our swift scene flies
In motion of no less celerity
Than that of thought.   Suppose that you have seen
The well-appointed king at Hampton pier   4
Embark his royalty; and his brave fleet
With silken streamers the young Phœbus fanning:

129 odds: *discord*   136 greener: *younger*
137 masters: *possesses*   145 breath: *breathing space*
1 imagin'd wing: *wings of imagination*   5 brave: *fine*

Play with your fancies, and in them behold
Upon the hempen tackle ship-boys climbing;   8
Hear the shrill whistle which doth order give
To sounds confus'd; behold the threaden sails,
Borne with the invisible and creeping wind,
Draw the huge bottoms through the furrow'd sea,   12
Breasting the lofty surge. O! do but think
You stand upon the rivage and behold
A city on the inconstant billows dancing;
For so appears this fleet majestical,   16
Holding due course to Harfleur. Follow, follow!
Grapple your minds to sternage of this navy,
And leave your England, as dead midnight still,
Guarded with grandsires, babies, and old women,   20
Either past or not arriv'd to pith and puissance:
For who is he, whose chin is but enrich'd
With one appearing hair, that will not follow
Those cull'd and choice-drawn cavaliers to France? 24
Work, work your thoughts, and therein see a siege;
Behold the ordnance on their carriages,
With fatal mouths gaping on girded Harfleur.
Suppose the ambassador from the French comes
    back;   28
Tells Harry that the king doth offer him
Katharine his daughter; and with her, to dowry,
Some petty and unprofitable dukedoms:
The offer likes not: and the nimble gunner   32
With linstock now the devilish cannon touches,
        Alarum, and chambers go off.
And down goes all before them. Still be kind,
And eke out our performance with your mind.
                          Exit.

14 rivage: *shore*   18 to sternage: *astern*   27 girded: *besieged*
32 likes: *pleases*   33 linstock: *stick to hold the gunner's match*
S. d. Alarum: *call to arms*   chambers: *small cannon*

Henry stirs the
English to
patriotism

Scene One

[*France.   Before Harfleur*]

Enter the King, Exeter, Bedford, and Gloucester.
Alarum: scaling ladders.

K. Hen. Once more unto the breach, dear friends,
      once more;
Or close the wall up with our English dead!
In peace there's nothing so becomes a man
As modest stillness and humility: 4
But when the blast of war blows in our ears,
Then imitate the action of the tiger;
Stiffen the sinews, summon up the blood,
Disguise fair nature with hard-favour'd rage;   8
Then lend the eye a terrible aspect;
Let it pry through the portage of the head
Like the brass cannon; let the brow o'erwhelm it
As fearfully as doth a galled rock   12
O'erhang and jutty his confounded base,
Swill'd with the wild and wasteful ocean.
Now set the teeth and stretch the nostril wide,
Hold hard the breath, and bend up every spirit
To his full height! On, on, you noblest English!   17
Whose blood is fet from fathers of war-proof;
Fathers that, like so many Alexanders,
Have in these parts from morn till even fought,
And sheath'd their swords for lack of argument.   21
Dishonour not your mothers; now attest
That those whom you call'd fathers did beget you.
Be copy now to men of grosser blood,   24

8 hard-favour'd: *ugly*   10 portage: *porthole*
11 o'erwhelm: *overhang*   12 galled: *undermined*
13 jutty: *project beyond*   confounded: *ruined*
14 Swill'd with: *gulped down by*
18 fet: *fetched*   war-proof: *valor proven in war*
21 argument: *subject of contention*   24 copy: *example*

arousing them by complement-
ing them.

And teach them how to war. And you, good yeomen,
Whose limbs were made in England, show us here
The mettle of your pasture; let us swear
That you are worth your breeding; which I doubt
  not;   28
For there is none of you so mean and base
That hath not noble lustre in your eyes.
I see you stand like greyhounds in the slips,
Straining upon the start. The game's afoot: 32
Follow your spirit; and, upon this charge
Cry 'God for Harry, England, and Saint George!'
   [*Exeunt.*] *Alarum, and chambers go off.*

Scene Two

[*The Same*]

Enter Nym, Bardolph, Pistol, and Boy.

 Bard. On, on, on, on, on! to the breach, to
the breach!

 Nym. Pray thee, corporal, stay: the knocks
are too hot; and for mine own part, I have not 4
a case of lives: the humour of it is too hot, that
is the very plain-song of it.

 Pist. The plain-song is most just, for hu-
mours do abound: 8
'Knocks go and come: God's vassals drop and die;
   And sword and shield
   In bloody field
   Doth win immortal fame.'   12

 Boy. Would I were in an alehouse in London!
I would give all my fame for a pot of ale, and
safety.

27 mettle of your pasture: *quality of your rearing*
31 in the slips: *in leash*   3 corporal; *cf. n.*
5 case: *set*   6 plain-song: *simple truth; cf. n.*

Pist. And I: 16

   'If wishes would prevail with me,
     My purpose should not fail with me,
      But thither would I hie.'
   Boy.   'As duly,   20
      But not as truly,
      As bird doth sing on bough.'

   Enter Fluellen and beats them in.

Flu. Up to the breach, you dogs! avaunt, you cullions!

Pist. Be merciful, great duke, to men of mould!   24
Abate thy rage, abate thy manly rage!
Abate thy rage, great duke!
Good bawcock, bate thy rage; use lenity, sweet chuck!

   Nym. These be good humours! your honour
wins bad humours.

            Exit [*with Pistol and Bardolph*].

   Boy. [*Aside.*] As young as I am, I have ob-
served these three swashers. I am boy to them
all three, but all they three, though they would
serve me, could not be man to me; for indeed
three such antics do not amount to a man. For   34
Bardolph, he is white-livered and red-faced; by
the means whereof, a' faces it out, but fights not.
For Pistol, he hath a killing tongue and a quiet
sword; by the means whereof a' breaks words,
and keeps whole weapons. For Nym, he hath
heard that men of few words are the best men; 40
and therefore he scorns to say his prayers, lest a'
should be thought a coward: but his few bad words

23 cullions: *wretches*
24 men of mould: *men of earth; i.e., mere mortals*
27 bawcock, chuck: *terms of endearment*   31 swashers: *braggarts*
34 antics: *buffoons*

[handwritten marginalia: describes Bardolph 'in appearance; Pistol 'in talking; Nym 'in neither appearance nor speech.]

are matched with as few good deeds; for a' never
broke any man's head but his own, and that was 44
against a post when he was drunk. They will
steal any thing and call it purchase. Bardolph
stole a lute-case, bore it twelve leagues, and sold
it for three half-pence. Nym and Bardolph are 48
sworn brothers in filching, and in Calais they
stole a fire-shovel: I knew by that piece of service the men would carry coals. They would
have me as familiar with men's pockets as their 52
gloves or their handkerchers: which makes
much against my manhood if I should take
from another's pocket to put into mine; for it is
plain pocketing up of wrongs. I must leave them 56
and seek some better service: their villainy goes
against my weak stomach, and therefore I must
cast it up.   *Exit.*

Enter Gower.

Gow. Captain Fluellen, you must come presently to the mines: the Duke of Gloucester
would speak with you.   62

Flu. To the mines! tell you the duke it is
not so good to come to the mines. For look
you, the mines is not according to the disciplines
of the war; the concavities of it is not sufficient; 66
for, look you, th' athversary—you may discuss
unto the duke, look you—is digt himself four
yard under the countermines; by Cheshu, I
think, a' will plow up all if there is not better
directions.   71

Gow. The Duke of Gloucester, to whom the

46 purchase: *slang term for money gained by cheating*
51 carry coals: *swallow insults*   65 the mines is not; *cf. n.*
67 discuss: *explain*   69 Cheshu: *Jesu*

order of the siege is given, is altogether directed
by an Irishman, a very valiant gentleman, i'
faith.

Flu. It is Captain Macmorris, is it not?   76
Gow. I think it be.

Flu. By Cheshu, he is an ass, as in the world:
I will verify as much in his beard: he has no
more directions in the true disciplines of the
wars, look you, of the Roman disciplines, than
is a puppy-dog.   82

Enter Macmorris and Captain Jamy.

Gow. Here a' comes; and the Scots captain,
Captain Jamy, with him.

Flu. Captain Jamy is a marvellous falorous
gentleman, that is certain; and of great expedi- 86
tion and knowledge in th' aunchient wars, upon
my particular knowledge of his directions: by
Cheshu, he will maintain his argument as well
as any military man in the world, in the disciplines of the pristine wars of the Romans.   91

Jamy. I say gud day, Captain Fluellen.

Flu. God-den to your worship, good Captain
James.

Gow. How now, Captain Macmorris! have
you quit the mines? have the pioners given o'er? 96

Mac. By Chrish, la! tish ill done: the work
ish give over, the trumpet sound the retreat. By
my hand, I swear, and my father's soul, the
work ish ill done; it ish give over: I would have
blowed up the town, so Chrish save me, la! in an
hour: O! tish ill done, tish ill done; by my
hand, tish ill done!   103

Flu. Captain Macmorris, I beseech you now, will you voutsafe me, look you, a few disputations with you, as partly touching or concerning the disciplines of the war, the Roman wars, in the way of argument, look you, and friendly communication; partly to satisfy my opinion, and partly for the satisfaction, look you, of my mind, as touching the direction of the military discipline: that is the point.   112

Jamy. It sall be vary gud, gud feith, gud captains bath: and I sall quit you with gud leve, as I may pick occasion; that sall I, marry.

Mac. It is no time to discourse, so Chrish save me: the day is hot, and the weather, and the wars, and the king, and the dukes: it is no time to discourse. The town is beseeched, and 119 the trumpet call us to the breach; and we talk, and be Chrish, do nothing: 'tis shame for us all; so God sa' me, 'tis shame to stand still; it is shame, by my hand; and there is throats to be cut, and works to be done; and there ish nothing done, so Chrish sa' me, la!   125

Jamy. By the mess, ere theise eyes of mine take themselves to slumber, aiie do gud service, or aile lig i' the grund for it; ay, or go to death; and aile pay 't as valorously as I may, that sal I suerly do, that is the breff and the long. Marry, I wad full fain heard some question 'tween you tway.   132

Flu. Captain Macmorris, I think, look you, under your correction, there is not many of your nation—   135

115 marry: *originally an oath by the Virgin Mary*
119 beseeched: *i.e., besieged*   122 sa': *save*
126 mess: *Mass*   128 lig: *lie*   132 tway: *two*

Mac. Of my nation! What ish my nation? ish a villain, and a bastard, and a knave, and a rascal? What ish my nation? Who talks of my nation?   139

Flu. Look you, if you take the matter otherwise than is meant, Captain Macmorris, peradventure I shall think you do not use me with that affability as in discretion you ought to use me, look you; being as good a man as yourself, both in the disciplines of war, and in the derivation of my birth, and in other particularities.   146

Mac. I do not know you so good a man as myself: so Chrish save me, I will cut off your head.   149

Gow. Gentlemen both, you will mistake each other.

Jamy. A! that's a foul fault.   *A parley.*

Gow. The town sounds a parley.   153

Flu. Captain Macmorris, when there is more better opportunity to be required, look you, I will be so bold as to tell you I know the disciplines of war; and there is an end.

          Exit [*with Gower and the other captains*].

Scene Three

[*Before the Gates of Harfleur*]

[*The Governor and some Citizens on the walls; the English forces below.*]   *Enter the King and all his Train before the gates.*

K. Hen. How yet resolves the governor of the town?

136-139 Of my . . . nation; *cf. n.*

This is the latest parle we will admit:
Therefore to our best mercy give yourselves;
Or like to men proud of destruction
Defy us to our worst: for, as I am a soldier,—   4
A name that in my thoughts becomes me best,—
If I begin the battery once again,
I will not leave the half-achieved Harfleur
Till in her ashes she lie buried.   8
The gates of mercy shall be all shut up,
And the flesh'd soldier, rough and hard of heart,
In liberty of bloody hand shall range   12
With conscience wide as hell, mowing like grass
Your fresh-fair virgins and your flowering infants.
What is it then to me, if impious war,
Array'd in flames like to the prince of fiends,   16
Do, with his smirch'd complexion, all fell feats
Enlink'd to waste and desolation?
What is 't to me, when you yourselves are cause,
If your pure maidens fall into the hand   20
Of hot and forcing violation?
What rein can hold licentious wickedness
When down the hill he holds his fierce career?
We may as bootless spend our vain command
Upon the enraged soldiers in their spoil   25
As send precepts to the leviathan
To come ashore.   Therefore, you men of Harfleur,
Take pity of your town and of your people,   28
Whiles yet my soldiers are in my command;
Whiles yet the cool and temperate wind of grace
O'erblows the filthy and contagious clouds
Of heady murder, spoil, and villainy.   32

Saying down of the law to the French.

2 parle: *parley*
11 flesh'd: *hardened by bloodshed*
17 fell feats: *savage practices*
18 Enlink'd to: *associated with*
24 bootless: *uselessly*
31 O'erblows: *blows away*
32 heady: *headstrong*

If not, why, in a moment, look to see
The blind and bloody soldier with foul hand
Defile the locks of your shrill-shrieking daughters;
Your fathers taken by the silver beards,   36
And their most reverend heads dash'd to the walls;
Your naked infants spitted upon pikes,
Whiles the mad mothers with their howls confus'd
Do break the clouds, as did the wives of Jewry
At Herod's bloody-hunting slaughtermen.   41
What say you? will you yield, and this avoid?
Or, guilty in defence, be thus destroy'd?

    Gov. Our expectation hath this day an end.
The Dauphin, whom of succour we entreated,   45
Returns us that his powers are yet not ready
To raise so great a siege. Therefore, great king,
We yield our town and lives to thy soft mercy.
Enter our gates; dispose of us and ours;   49
For we no longer are defensible.

    K. Hen. Open your gates! Come, uncle Exeter,
Go you and enter Harfleur; there remain,   52
And fortify it strongly 'gainst the French:
Use mercy to them all. For us, dear uncle,
The winter coming on and sickness growing
Upon our soldiers, we will retire to Calais.   56
To-night in Harfleur will we be your guest;
To-morrow for the march are we addrest.

                 Flourish, and enter the town.

40 Jewry: *Judea; cf. St. Matthew 2. 16-18.*   45 of: *for*
46 Returns: *answers*   50 defensible: *capable of resisting*
58 addrest: *prepared*

[Handwritten marginal notes:]
He is scaring them to surrender
When he gains Entrance he immediately changes into his true self.

Scene Four

[*The French King's Palace*]

Enter Katharine and [Alice,] an old gentlewoman.

Kath. Alice, tu as été en Angleterre, et tu parles bien le langage.

Alice. Un peu, madame.　　　　3

Kath. Je te prie, m'enseignez; il faut que j'apprenne à parler. Comment appelez-vous la main en anglais?

Alice. La main? elle est appelée, de hand.

Kath. De hand. Et les doigts?　　　　8

Alice. Les doigts? ma foi, j'oublie les doigts; mais je me souviendrai. Les doigts? je pense qu'ils sont appelés de fingres; oui, de fingres.　　　　12

Kath. La main, de hand; les doigts, de fingres. Je pense que je suis le bon écolier; j'ai gagné deux mots d'anglais vîtement. Comment appelez-vous les ongles?　　　　16

Alice. Les ongles? nous les appelons, de nails.

Kath. De nails. Écoutez; dites-moi, si je parle bien: de hands, de fingres, et de nails.

Alice. C'est bien dit, madame; il est fort bon anglais.　　　　21

Kath. Dites-moi l'anglais pour le bras.

Alice. De arm, madame.

Kath. Et le coude?　　　　24

Alice. De elbow.

Kath. De elbow. Je m'en fais la répétition de tous les mots que vous m'avez appris dès à présent.　　　　28

Alice. Il est trop difficile, madame, comme je pense.

Kath. Excusez-moi, Alice; écoutez: de hand, de fingres, de nails, de arma, de bilbow.   32

Alice. De elbow, madame.

Kath. O Seigneur Dieu! je m'en oublie; de elbow.   Comment appelez-vous le col?

Alice. De nick, madame.   36

Kath. De nick.   Et le menton?

Alice. De chin.

Kath. De sin.   Le col, de nick: le menton, de sin.   40

Alice. Oui.   Sauf votre honneur, en vérité, vous prononcez les mots aussi droit que les natifs d'Angleterre.

Kath. Je ne doute point d'apprendre, par la grace de Dieu, et en peu de temps.   45

Alice. N'avez-vous pas déjà oublié ce que je vous ai enseigné?

Kath. Non, je reciterai à vous promptement: De hand, de fingre, de mails,—   49

Alice. De nails, madame.

Kath. De nails, de arme, de ilbow.

Alice. Sauf votre honneur, de elbow.   52

Kath. Ainsi dis-je; de elbow, de nick, et de sin.   Comment appelez-vous le pied et la robe?

Alice. De foot, madame; et de coun.   55

Kath. De foot, et de coun?   O Seigneur Dieu! ce sont mots de son mauvais, corruptible, gros, et impudique, et non pour les dames d'honneur d'user: je ne voudrais prononcer ces mots devant les seigneurs de France, pour tout le monde.   Foh! le foot, et le coun.   Néanmoins je réciterai une autre fois ma leçon ensemble: de hand, de fingre, de nails, de arm, de elbow, de nick, de sin, de foot, de coun.   64

these words in french are immoral

S. cleverly turns this seemingly innocent scene into a bawdy-

Alice. Excellent, madame!

Kath. C'est assez pour une fois: allons-nous
à dîner.   *Exit [with Alice].*

Scene Five

[*Rouen*]

*Enter the King of France, the Dauphin, [Duke of
Bourbon,] the Constable of France, and Others.*

Fr. King. 'Tis certain, he hath pass'd the river
  Somme.

Con. And if he be not fought withal, my lord,
Let us not live in France; let us quit all,
And give our vineyards to a barbarous people.   4

Dau. O Dieu vivant! shall a few sprays of us,
The emptying of our fathers' luxury,
Our scions, put in wild and savage stock,
Spirt up so suddenly into the clouds,   8
And overlook their grafters?

Bour. Normans, but bastard Normans, Norman
  bastards!
Mort de ma vie! if they march along
Unfought withal, but I will sell my dukedom,   12
To buy a slobbery and a dirty farm
In that nook-shotten isle of Albion.

Con. Dieu de batailles! where have they this
  mettle?
Is not their climate foggy, raw, and dull,   16
On whom, as in despite, the sun looks pale,
Killing their fruit with frowns? Can sodden water,
A drench for sur-rein'd jades, their barley-broth,

---

5 sprays: *branches*   6 emptying: *issue*   luxury: *lust*
7 scions; *cf. n.*   9 overlook: *rise above*   12 but; *cf. n.*
14 nook-shotten: *running out into promontories*
19 drench: *bran and water*   sur-rein'd jades: *over-ridden horses*
  barley-broth: *beer*

Decoct their cold blood to such valiant heat?   20
And shall our quick blood, spirited with wine,
Seem frosty? O! for honour of our land,
Let us not hang like roping icicles
Upon our houses' thatch, whiles a more frosty
    people   24
Sweat drops of gallant youth in our rich fields;
Poor we may call them in their native lords.

    Dau. By faith and honour,
Our madams mock at us, and plainly say   28
Our mettle is bred out; and they will give
Their bodies to the lust of English youth
To new-store France with bastard warriors.

    Bour. They bid us to the English dancing-
    schools,   32
And teach lavoltas high and swift corantos;
Saying our grace is only in our heels,
And that we are most lofty runaways.

    Fr. King. Where is Montjoy the herald? speed him
    hence: 36
Let him greet England with our sharp defiance.
Up, princes! and, with spirit of honour edg'd
More sharper than your swords, hie to the field:
Charles Delabreth, High Constable of France;   40
You Dukes of Orleans, Bourbon, and of Berri,
Alençon, Brabant, Bar, and Burgundy;
Jaques Chatillon, Rambures, Vaudemont,
Beaumont, Grandpré, Roussi, and Fauconberg,
Foix, Lestrale, Bouciqualt, and Charolois;   45
High dukes, great princes, barons, lords, and knights,
For your great seats now quit you of great shames.
Bar Harry England, that sweeps through our land

20 Decoct: *warm*   23 roping: *dripping*
33 lavoltas, corantos: *the names of certain lively dances*
36 Montjoy; *cf. n.*

With pennons painted in the blood of Harfleur:
Rush on his host, as doth the melted snow
Upon the valleys, whose low vassal seat
The Alps doth spit and void his rheum upon: 52
Go down upon him, you have power enough,
And in a captive chariot into Roan
Bring him our prisoner.
 Con.   This becomes the great.
Sorry am I his numbers are so few,   56
His soldiers sick and famish'd in their march,
For I am sure when he shall see our army
He'll drop his heart into the sink of fear,
And for achievement offer us his ransom.   60
 Fr. King. Therefore, lord constable, haste on Mont-
  joy,
And let him say to England that we send
To know what willing ransom he will give.
Prince Dauphin, you shall stay with us in Roan.
 Dau. Not so, I do beseech your majesty.   65
 Fr. King. Be patient, for you shall remain with us.
Now forth, lord constable and princes all,
And quickly bring us word of England's fall.   68
       Exeunt.

Scene Six

[*The English Camp in Picardy*]

Enter Captains, English and Welch, Gower and
Fluellen.

 Gow. How now, Captain Fluellen! come you
from the bridge?
 Flu. I assure you, there is very excellent
services committed at the pridge.

Gow. Is the Duke of Exeter safe?

Flu. The Duke of Exeter is as magnanimous
as Agamemnon; and a man that I love and
honour with my soul, and my heart, and my
duty, and my life, and my living, and my utter-
most power: he is not—God be praised and
plessed!—any hurt in the world; but keeps the 11
pridge most valiantly, with excellent discipline.
There is an aunchient lieutenant there at the
pridge, I think, in my very conscience, he is as
valiant a man as Mark Antony; and he is a man
of no estimation in the world; but I did see him
do as gallant service.   17

Gow. What do you call him?

Flu. He is called Aunchient Pistol.

Gow. I know him not.   20

Enter Pistol.

Flu. Here is the man.

Pist. Captain, I thee beseech to do me favours:
The Duke of Exeter doth love thee well.

Flu. Ay, I praise God; and I have merited
some love at his hands.   25

Pist. Bardolph, a soldier firm and sound of heart,
And of buxom valour, hath, by cruel fate
And giddy Fortune's furious fickle wheel,   28
That goddess blind,
That stands upon the rolling restless stone,—

Flu. By your patience, Aunchient Pistol. Fortune is painted plind, with a muffler afore her
eyes, to signify to you that Fortune is plind: and
she is painted also with a wheel, to signify to 34
you, which is the moral of it, that she is turning,

---

13 aunchient lieutenant; *cf. n.*   27 buxom: *brisk*

and inconstant, and mutability, and variation:
and her foot, look you, is fixed upon a spherical
stone, which rolls, and rolls, and rolls: in good
truth, the poet makes a most excellent description of it: Fortune is an excellent moral.   40

Pist. Fortune is Bardolph's foe, and frowns on
  him;
For he hath stol'n a pax, and hanged must a' be,
A damned death!
Let gallows gape for dog, let man go free   44
And let not hemp his wind-pipe suffocate.
But Exeter hath given the doom of death
For pax of little price.
Therefore, go speak; the duke will hear thy voice; 48
And let not Bardolph's vital thread be cut
With edge of penny cord and vile reproach:
Speak, captain, for his life, and I will thee requite.

Flu. Aunchient Pistol, I do partly understand your meaning.   53

Pist. Why then, rejoice therefore.

Flu. Certainly, aunchient, it is not a thing to
rejoice at; for, if, look you, he were my brother,
I would desire the duke to use his good pleasure
and put him to execution; for discipline ought
to be used.

Pist. Die and be damn'd; and figo for thy friendship!   60

Flu. It is well.

Pist. The fig of Spain!   *Exit.*

Flu. Very good.

Gow. Why, this is an arrant counterfeit
rascal: I remember him now; a bawd, a cutpurse.   66

42 pax; *cf. n.*   60 figo: *a fig*   62 The fig of Spain; *cf. n.*

Flu. I'll assure you a' uttered as prave words at the pridge as you shall see in a summer's day. But it is very well; what he has spoke to me, that is well, I warrant you, when time is serve.   71

Gow. Why, 'tis a gull, a fool, a rogue, that now and then goes to the wars to grace himself at his return into London under the form of a soldier. And such fellows are perfect in the 75 great commanders' names, and they will learn you by rote where services were done; at such and such a sconce, at such a breach, at such a convoy; who came off bravely, who was shot, who disgraced, what terms the enemy stood on; 80 and this they con perfectly in the phrase of war, which they trick up with new-tuned oaths: and what a beard of the general's cut and a horrid suit of the camp will do among foaming bottles 84 and ale-washed wits, is wonderful to be thought on. But you must learn to know such slanders of the age, or else you may be marvellously mistook.   88

Flu. I tell you what, Captain Gower; I do perceive, he is not the man that he would gladly make show to the world he is: if I find a hole in his coat I will tell him my mind. [*Drum heard.*] Hark you, the king is coming; and I must speak with him from the pridge.

Drum and Colours. Enter the King, [Gloucester,] and his poor Soldiers.

Flu. God pless your majesty!

72 gull: *cheat*   78 sconce: *small fort*
80 stood on: *insisted on*   94 from: *with news from*

K. Hen. How now, Fluellen! cam'st thou from the
    bridge?   96

Flu. Ay, so please your majesty.   The Duke
of Exeter hath very gallantly maintained the
pridge: the French is gone off, look you, and there
is gallant and most prave passages.   Marry, th' 100
athversary was have possession of the pridge,
but he is enforced to rctire, and the Duke of
Exeter is master of the pridge.   I can tell your
majesty the duke is a prave man.   104

K. Hen. What men have you lost, Fluellen?

Flu. The perdition of th' athversary hath been
very great, reasonable great: marry, for my
part, I think the duke hath lost never a man but
one that is like to be executed for robbing a 109
church; one Bardolph, if your majesty know the
man: his face is all bubukles, and whelks, and
knobs, and flames o' fire; and his lips blows at
his nose, and it is like a coal of fire, sometimes
plue and sometimes red; but his nose is exe-
cuted, and his fire's out.   115

K. Hen. We would have all such offenders so
cut off: and we give express charge that in our
marches through the country there be nothing
compelled from the villages, nothing taken but
paid for, none of the French upbraided or
abused in disdainful language; for when lenity
and cruelty play for a kingdom, the gentler
gamester is the soonest winner.

states policy re conduct of army.

         Tucket.   Enter Montjoy.

  Mont. You know me by my habit.   124

100 passages: *deeds*   106 perdition: *losses*
111 bubukles: *carbuncles*   whelks: *boils*
123 S. d. Tucket: *trumpet signal*   124 habit: *herald's coat*

K. Hen. Well then I know thee: what shall I
know of thee?

Mont. My master's mind.

K. Hen. Unfold it.   127

Mont. Thus says my king: Say thou to Harry
of England: Though we seemed dead, we did but
sleep: advantage is a better soldier than rash-
ness. Tell him, we could have rebuked him at
Harfleur, but that we thought not good to bruise
an injury till it were full ripe: now we speak 133
upon our cue, and our voice is imperial: England
shall repent his folly, see his weakness, and ad-
mire our sufferance. Bid him therefore consider
of his ransom; which must proportion the losses
we have borne, the subjects we have lost, the
disgrace we have digested; which, in weight to 139
re-answer, his pettiness would bow under. For
our losses, his exchequer is too poor; for the
effusion of our blood, the muster of his kingdom
too faint a number; and for our disgrace, his
own person, kneeling at our feet, but a weak and
worthless satisfaction. To this add defiance: and
tell him, for conclusion, he hath betrayed his
followers, whose condemnation is pronounced.
So far my king and master, so much my office.

K. Hen. What is thy name? I know thy quality.   149

Mont. Montjoy.

K. Hen. Thou dost thy office fairly. Turn thee
back,

And tell thy king I do not seek him now,   152

But could be willing to march on to Calais

125 of: *from*   134 upon our cue: *in proper time*
140 re-answer: *atone for*   149 quality: *profession*

Without impeachment; for, to say the sooth,—
Though 'tis no wisdom to confess so much
Unto an enemy of craft and vantage,—   156
My people are with sickness much enfeebled,
My numbers lessen'd, and those few I have
Almost no better than so many French:
Who, when they were in health, I tell thee, herald,   160
I thought upon one pair of English legs
Did march three Frenchmen. Yet, forgive me, God,
That I do brag thus! this your air of France
Hath blown that vice in me; I must repent.   164
Go therefore, tell thy master here I am:
My ransom is this frail and worthless trunk,
My army but a weak and sickly guard;
Yet, God before, tell him we will come on,   168
Though France himself and such another neighbour
Stand in our way. There's for thy labour, Montjoy.
Go, bid thy master well advise himself:
If we may pass, we will; if we be hinder'd,   172
We shall your tawny ground with your red blood
Discolour: and so, Montjoy, fare you well.
The sum of all our answer is but this:
We would not seek a battle as we are;   176
Nor, as we are, we say we will not shun it:
So tell your master.
   Mont. I shall deliver so. Thanks to your highness.
                               [*Exit.*]
   Glo. I hope they will not come upon us now.   180
   K. Hen. We are in God's hand, brother, not in
    theirs.
March to the bridge; it now draws toward night:

154 impeachment: *hindrance*   sooth: *truth*
156 of vantage: *favored by circumstances*
164 blown: *propagated*   179 deliver: *report*

Beyond the river we'll encamp ourselves,
And on to-morrow bid them march away.   184

Exeunt.

climatic scene Scene Seven
preceding
battle! [*The French Camp, near Agincourt*]

Enter the Constable of France, the Lord Rambures,
    [*the Duke of*] *Orleans,* [*the*] *Dauphin, with*
    Others.

S, altho' *Con.* Tut! I have the best armour of the
not a world. Would it were day!
soldier, *Orl.* You have an excellent armour; but let
my horse have his due.   4
seems *Con.* It is the best horse of Europe.
to know *Orl.* Will it never be morning?
how men *Dau.* My Lord of Orleans, and my lord high
feel before constable, you talk of horse and armour—   8
Orl. You are as well provided of both as any
a battle! prince in the world.

Dau. What a long night is this! I will not
change my horse with any that treads but on   12
four pasterns. Ça, ha! He bounds from the
earth as if his entrails were hairs: le cheval
volant, the Pegasus, chez les narines de feu!
When I bestride him, I soar, I am a hawk: he 16
trots the air; the earth sings when he touches
it; the basest horn of his hoof is more musical
than the pipe of Hermes.

Orl. He's of the colour of the nutmeg.   20

Dau. And of the heat of the ginger. It is a
beast for Perseus: he is pure air and fire; and
the dull elements of earth and water never

14 as if . . . hairs: *i.e., as if he were a tennis ball; cf. n.*
15 chez: *i.e., with*   19 pipe of Hermes; *cf. n.*

appear in him but only in patient stillness while 24
his rider mounts him: he is indeed a horse; and
all other jades you may call beasts.

Con. Indeed, my lord, it is a most absolute
and excellent horse.   28

Dau. It is the prince of palfreys; his neigh
is like the bidding of a monarch and his counte-
nance enforces homage.

Orl. No more, cousin.   32

Dau. Nay, the man hath no wit that cannot,
from the rising of the lark to the lodging of the
lamb, vary deserved praise on my palfrey: it is
a theme as fluent as the sea; turn the sands into 36
eloquent tongues, and my horse is argument for
them all. 'Tis a subject for a sovereign to reason on, and for a sovereign's sovereign to ride
on; and for the world—familiar to us, and 40
unknown—to lay apart their particular functions and wonder at him. I once writ a sonnet in his praise and began thus: 'Wonder of
nature!'—   44

Orl. I have heard a sonnet begin so to one's
mistress.

Dau. Then did they imitate that which I
composed to my courser; for my horse is my
mistress.   49

Orl. Your mistress bears well.

Dau. Me well; which is the prescript praise
and perfection of a good and particular mis-
tress.   53

Con. Nay, for methought yesterday your mistress shrewdly shook your back.

27 absolute: *perfect*   34 lodging: *lying down*
37 argument: *theme*   51 prescript: *prescribed*
55 shrewdly: *viciously*

Dau. So perhaps did yours.   56

Con. Mine was not bridled.

Dau. O! then belike she was old and gentle;
and you rode, like a kern of Ireland, your French
hose off and in your straight strossers.   60

Con. You have good judgment in horseman-
ship.

Dau. Be warned by me, then: they that ride
so, and ride not warily, fall into foul bogs. I
had rather have my horse to my mistress.   65

Con. I had as lief have my mistress a jade.

Dau. I tell thee, constable, my mistress wears
his own hair.   68

Con. I could make as true a boast as that if I
had a sow to my mistress.

Dau. 'Le chien est retourné à son propre
vomissement, et la truie lavée au bourbier': thou
makest use of any thing.   73

Con. Yet do I not use my horse for my mistress: or any such proverb so little kin to the
purpose.   76

Ram. My lord constable, the armour that I
saw in your tent to-night, are those stars or
suns upon it?

Con. Stars, my lord.   80

Dau. Some of them will fall to-morrow, I
hope.

Con. And yet my sky shall not want.

Dau. That may be, for you bear a many
superfluously, and 'twere more honour some
were away.   86

Con. Even as your horse bears your praises;

---

59 kern: *light-armed Irish soldier*   59, 60 French hose: *wide breeches*
60 straight strossers: *tight trousers*   65 to: *as*
71, 72 *Cf. n.*

who would trot as well were some of your brags
dismounted.   89

Dau. Would I were able to load him with his
desert! Will it never be day? I will trot to-
morrow a mile, and my way shall be paved with
English faces.   93

Con. I will not say so for fear I should be
faced out of my way. But I would it were
morning, for I would fain be about the ears of
the English.   97

Ram. Who will go to hazard with me for
twenty prisoners?

Con. You must first go yourself to hazard,
ere you have them.   101

Dau. 'Tis midnight: I'll go arm myself.   *Exit.*

Orl. The Dauphin longs for morning.

Ram. He longs to eat the English.   104

Con. I think he will eat all he kills.

Orl. By the white hand of my lady, he's a
gallant prince.

Con. Swear by her foot, that she may tread
out the oath.   109

Orl. He is simply the most active gentleman
of France.

Con. Doing is activity, and he will still be
doing.   113

Orl. He never did harm, that I heard of.

Con. Nor will do none to-morrow: he will
keep that good name still.   116

Orl. I know him to be valiant.

Con. I was told that by one that knows him
better than you.

Orl. What's he?   120

95 faced out of my way: *outfaced (put to shame)*
98 go to hazard: *throw at dice; cf. n.*

Con. Marry, he told me so himself; and he said he cared not who knew it.

Orl. He needs not; it is no hidden virtue in him. 124

Con. By my faith, sir, but it is; never anybody saw it but his lackey: 'tis a hooded valour; and when it appears, it will bate.

Orl. 'Ill will never said well.' 128

Con. I will cap that proverb with 'There is flattery in friendship.'

Orl. And I will take up that with 'Give the devil his due.' 132

Con. Well placed: there stands your friend for the devil: have at the very eye of that proverb, with 'A pox of the devil.'

Orl. You are the better at proverbs, by how much 'A fool's bolt is soon shot.' 137

Con. You have shot over.

Orl. 'Tis not the first time you were overshot.

Enter a Messenger.

Mess. My lord high constable, the English lie within fifteen hundred paces of your tents. 141

Con. Who hath measured the ground?

Mess. The Lord Grandpré.

Con. A valiant and most expert gentleman. Would it were day! Alas! poor Harry of England, he longs not for the dawning as we do. 146

Orl. What a wretched and peevish fellow is this King of England, to mope with his fatbrained followers so far out of his knowledge!

126 'tis a hooded valour; *cf. n.*
139 overshot: *beaten at shooting (with a pun on 'drunk')*
147 peevish: *foolish*   149 out . . . knowledge: *beyond his depth*

Con. If the English had any apprehension
they would run away.   151

Orl. That they lack; for if their heads had
any intellectual armour they could never wear
such heavy head-pieces.

Ram. That island of England breeds very
valiant creatures: their mastiffs are of un-
matchable courage.   157

Orl. Foolish curs! that run winking into the
mouth of a Russian bear and have their heads
crushed like rotten apples. You may as well say
that's a valiant flea that dare eat his breakfast
on the lip of a lion.   162

Con. Just, just; and the men do sympathize
with the mastiffs in robustious and rough coming on, leaving their wits with their wives: and
then give them great meals of beef and iron
and steel, they will eat like wolves and fight
like devils.   168

Orl. Ay, but these English are shrewdly out
of beef.

Con. Then shall we find to-morrow they have
only stomachs to eat and none to fight. Now is
it time to arm; come, shall we about it?   173

Orl. It is now two o'clock: but, let me see, by ten
We shall have each a hundred Englishmen. *Exeunt.*

150 apprehension: *intelligence*   163 sympathize with: *resemble*
164 robustious: *sturdy*

supreme speech
to further establish
the atmosphere.

ACT FOURTH

Chorus.

Now entertain conjecture of a time
When creeping murmur and the poring dark
Fills the wide vessel of the universe.
From camp to camp, through the foul womb of
    night,   4
The hum of either army stilly sounds,
That the fix'd sentinels almost receive
The secret whispers of each other's watch:

Enemy
camps
are so
near,
voices
& sounds
of ani-
mals
can be
heard,

Fire answers fire, and through their paly flames   8
Each battle sees the other's umber'd face:
Steed threatens steed, in high and boastful neighs
Piercing the night's dull ear; and from the tents
The armourers, accomplishing the knights,   12
With busy hammers closing rivets up,
Give dreadful note of preparation.
The country cocks do crow, the clocks do toll,
And the third hour of drowsy morning name.   16
Proud of their numbers, and secure in soul,
The confident and over-lusty French
Do the low-rated English play at dice;
And chide the cripple-tardy-gaited night   20
Who, like a foul and ugly witch, doth limp
So tediously away.   The poor condemned English,
Like sacrifices, by their watchful fires
Sit patiently, and inly ruminate   24
The morning's danger, and their gesture sad
Investing lank-lean cheeks and war-worn coats
Presenteth them unto the gazing moon
So many horrid ghosts.   O now, who will behold   28

2 poring: *dim-sighted*   5 stilly: *softly*
9 battle: *army*   umber'd: *dusky*   12 accomplishing: *equipping*
18 over-lusty: *overconfident*   19 play: *play for*
25 gesture: *bearing*   26 Investing: *accompanying*

The royal captain of this ruin'd band
Walking from watch to watch, from tent to tent,
Let him cry 'Praise and glory on his head!'
For forth he goes and visits all his host,   32
Bids them good morrow with a modest smile,
And calls them brothers, friends, and countrymen.
Upon his royal face there is no note
How dread an army hath enrounded him;   36
Nor doth he dedicate one jot of colour
Unto the weary and all-watched night:
But freshly looks and overbears attaint
With cheerful semblance and sweet majesty;   40
That every wretch, pining and pale before,
Beholding him, plucks comfort from his looks.
A largess universal, like the sun,
His liberal eye doth give to every one,   44
Thawing cold fear, that mean and gentle all
Behold, as may unworthiness define,
A little touch of Harry in the night.
And so our scene must to the battle fly;   48
Where,—O for pity,—we shall much disgrace,
With four or five most vile and ragged foils,
Right ill dispos'd in brawl ridiculous,
The name of Agincourt. Yet sit and see,   52
Minding true things by what their mockeries be.

                                                    Exit.

Scene One

[*The English Camp at Agincourt*]

Enter the King, Bedford, and Gloucester.

   K. Hen. Gloucester, 'tis true that we are in great
      danger;

36 enrounded: *surrounded*   39 overbears attaint: *subdues anxiety*
46 as . . . define: *so far as they are able to apprehend*
53 Minding: *imagining*

Hen, walks thru the camp, talking with of his men.

The greater therefore should our courage be.
Good morrow, brother Bedford. God Almighty!
There is some soul of goodness in things evil,   4
Would men observingly distil it out;
For our bad neighbour makes us early stirrers,
Which is both healthful, and good husbandry:
Besides, they are our outward consciences,   8
And preachers to us all; admonishing
That we should dress us fairly for our end.
Thus may we gather honey from the weed,
And make a moral of the devil himself.   12

Enter Erpingham.

Good morrow, old Sir Thomas Erpingham:
A good soft pillow for that good white head
Were better than a churlish turf of France.
   Erp. Not so, my liege: this lodging likes me
     better,   16
Since I may say, 'Now lie I like a king.'
   K. Hen. 'Tis good for men to love their present
     pains
Upon example; so the spirit is eas'd:
And when the mind is quicken'd, out of doubt,   20
The organs, though defunct and dead before,
Break up their drowsy grave, and newly move
With casted slough and fresh legerity.
Lend me thy cloak, Sir Thomas. Brothers both,
Commend me to the princes in our camp;   25
Do my good morrow to them; and anon
Desire them all to my pavilion.
   Glo. We shall, my liege.   28

10 dress us: *prepare ourselves*
19 Upon example: *by virtue of the example set by another*
20 out of doubt: *certainly*
23 casted slough: *cast-off skin (of a snake)*   legerity: *alacrity*
27 Desire: *summon*

Erp. Shall I attend your Grace?

K. Hen.   No, my good knight;

Go with my brothers to my lords of England:

I and my bosom must debate awhile,

And then I would no other company.   32

Erp. The Lord in heaven bless thee, noble Harry!

               Exeunt [all but the King].

K. Hen. God-a-mercy, old heart! thou speak'st cheerfully.

            Enter Pistol.

Pist. Che vous la?

K. Hen. A friend.   36

Pist. Discuss unto me; art thou officer?

Or art thou base, common and popular?

K. Hen. I am a gentleman of a company.

Pist. Trail'st thou the puissant pike?   40

K. Hen. Even so. What are you?

Pist. As good a gentleman as the emperor.

K. Hen. Then you are a better than the king.

Pist. The king's a bawcock, and a heart of gold,   44

A lad of life, an imp of fame:

Of parents good, of fist most valiant:

I kiss his dirty shoe, and from heart-string

I love the lovely bully. What's thy name?   48

K. Hen. Harry le Roy.

Pist. Le Roy! a Cornish name: art thou of Cornish crew?

K. Hen. No, I am a Welshman. ——Prince of Wales.

Pist. Know'st thou Fluellen?   52

K. Hen. Yes.

Pist. Tell him, I'll knock his leek about his pate

Upon Saint Davy's day.

35 Che vous la: *i.e., Qui va là*   38 popular: *plebeian*

45 imp: *youngling*   48 bully: *good fellow*

55 Saint Davy's day: *March 1; cf. n.*

K. Hen. Do not you wear your dagger in your
cap that day, lest he knock that about yours.   57
Pist. Art thou his friend?
K. Hen. And his kinsman too.
Pist. The figo for thee then!   60
K. Hen. I thank you.   God be with you!
Pist. My name is Pistol called.   *Exit.*
K. Hen. It sorts well with your fierceness.

 Enter Fluellen and Gower [severally].

Gow. Captain Fluellen!   64
Flu. So! in the name of Cheshu Christ, speak
lower.   It is the greatest admiration in the
universal world, when the true and auncient
prerogatifes and laws of the wars is not kept.
If you would take the pains but to examine the
wars of Pompey the Great, you shall find, I
warrant you, that there is no tiddle-taddle nor
pibble-pabble in Pompey's camp; I warrant
you, you shall find the ceremonies of the wars,
and the cares of it, and the forms of it, and the
sobriety of it, and the modesty of it, to be otherwise.   76
Gow. Why, the enemy is loud; you hear
him all night.
Flu. If the enemy is an ass and a fool and a
prating coxcomb, is it meet, think you, that we
should also, look you, be an ass and a fool and a
prating coxcomb, in your own conscience now?
 Gow. I will speak lower.   83
 Flu. I pray you and peseech you that you
will.   *Exit [with Gower].*
K. Hen. Though it appear a little out of fashion,
There is much care and valour in this Welshman.

59 kinsman: *brother Welshman (Henry was born at Monmouth)*

Enter three soldiers: John Bates, Alexander Court,
and Michael Williams.

Court. Brother John Bates, is not that the
morning which breaks yonder?   89

Bates. I think it be; but we have no great
cause to desire the approach of day.

Will. We see yonder the beginning of the
day, but I think we shall never see the end of
it. Who goes there?

K. Hen. A friend.

Will. Under what captain serve you?   96

K. Hen. Under Sir Thomas Erpingham.

Will. A good old commander and a most
kind gentleman: I pray you, what thinks he of
our estate?   100

K. Hen. Even as men wrecked upon a sand,
that look to be washed off the next tide.

Bates. He hath not told his thought to the
king?   104

K. Hen. No; nor it is not meet he should.
For, though I speak it to you, I think the king
is but a man, as I am: the violet smells to him
as it doth to me; the element shows to him as
it doth to me; all his senses have but human
conditions: his ceremonies laid by, in his naked-
ness he appears but a man; and though his 111
affections are higher mounted than ours, yet
when they stoop, they stoop with the like wing.
Therefore when he sees reason of fears, as we do,
his fears, out of doubt, be of the same relish as

100 estate: *position*   101 sand: *sand-bank*
108 element: *sky*   shows: *appears*
110 ceremonies: *marks of office*
113 stoop: *term of falconry, used of the hawk descending on its prey*
115 relish: *flavor*

ours are: yet, in reason, no man should possess
him with any appearance of fear, lest he, by
showing it, should dishearten his army.   118

Bates. He may show what outward courage
he will, but I believe, as cold a night as 'tis, he
could wish himself in Thames up to the neck,
and so I would he were, and I by him, at all
adventures, so we were quit here.   123

K. Hen. By my troth, I will speak my conscience of the king: I think he would not wish
himself anywhere but where he is.

Bates. Then I would he were here alone; so
should he be sure to be ransomed, and a many
poor men's lives saved.   129

K. Hen. I dare say you love him not so ill
to wish him here alone, howsoever you speak
this to feel other men's minds.   Methinks I
could not die anywhere so contented as in the
king's company, his cause being just and his
quarrel honourable.

Will. That's more than we know.   136

Bates. Ay, or more than we should seek after;
for we know enough if we know we are the king's
subjects.   If his cause be wrong, our obedience
to the king wipes the crime of it out of us.   140

Will. But if the cause be not good, the king
himself hath a heavy reckoning to make; when
all those legs and arms and heads, chopped off
in a battle, shall join together at the latter day,
and cry all, 'We died at such a place'; some
swearing, some crying for a surgeon, some upon
their wives left poor behind them, some upon
the debts they owe, some upon their children

116 possess: *infect*   116 possess: *infect*   124 conscience: *private opinion*

rawly left. I am afeard there are few die well 149
that die in a battle; for how can they charitably
dispose of anything when blood is their argument? Now, if these men do not die well, it
will be a black matter for the king that led them
to it, who to disobey were against all proportion of subjection.   155

K. Hen. So, if a son that is by his father sent
about merchandise do sinfully miscarry upon
the sea, the imputation of his wickedness, by
your rule, should be imposed upon his father,
that sent him: or if a servant, under his master's
command transporting a sum of money, be as-
sailed by robbers and die in many irreconciled 162
iniquities, you may call the business of the master
the author of the servant's damnation. But this
is not so: the king is not bound to answer the
particular endings of his soldiers, the father of
his son, nor the master of his servant; for they
purpose not their death when they purpose their
services. Besides, there is no king, be his cause
never so spotless, if it come to the arbitrement 170
of swords, can try it out with all unspotted soldiers. Some, peradventure, have on them the
guilt of premeditated and contrived murder;
some, of beguiling virgins with the broken seals
of perjury; some, making the wars their bul-
wark, that have before gored the gentle bosom
of peace with pillage and robbery. Now, if these
men have defeated the law and outrun native 178
punishment, though they can outstrip men, they

149 rawly: *without due provision*   151 argument: *business*
154, 155 all . . . subjection: *all that is reasonably demanded of a subject*
                                             157 miscarry: *perish*
162 irreconciled: *unatoned for*   170 arbitrement: *decision*
173 contrived: *plotted*   178 native: *in their home country*

have no wings to fly from God: war is his beadle,
war is his vengeance; so that here men are
punished for before-breach of the king's laws in
now the king's quarrel: where they feared the
death they have borne life away, and where they
would be safe they perish.   Then, if they die 185
unprovided, no more is the king guilty of their
damnation than he was before guilty of those
impieties for the which they are now visited.
Every subject's duty is the king's; but every
subject's soul is his own.   Therefore should every
soldier in the wars do as every sick man in his
bed, wash every mote out of his conscience; and
dying so, death is to him advantage; or not 193
dying, the time was blessedly lost wherein such
preparation was gained: and in him that es-
capes, it were not sin to think, that making God
so free an offer, he let him outlive that day to
see his greatness, and to teach others how they
should prepare.   199

Will. 'Tis certain, every man that dies ill, the
ill upon his own head: the king is not to answer
it.

Bates. I do not desire he should answer for
me; and yet I determine to fight lustily for him.

K. Hen. I myself heard the king say he would
not be ransomed.   206

Will. Ay, he said so, to make us fight cheerfully; but when our throats are cut he may be
ransomed, and we ne'er the wiser.

K. Hen. If I live to see it, I will never trust
his word after.   211

Will. You pay him then.   That's a perilous

180 beadle: *minor police officer*
186 unprovided: *unprepared*
                                      212 pay: *punish*

shot out of an elder-gun, that a poor and a
private displeasure can do against a monarch.
You may as well go about to turn the sun to
ice with fanning in his face with a peacock's
feather. You'll never trust his word after!
come, 'tis a foolish saying.   218

K. Hen. Your reproof is something too round;
I should be angry with you if the time were con-
venient.   221

Will. Let it be a quarrel between us, if you
live.

K. Hen. I embrace it.   224

Will. How shall I know thee again?

K. Hen. Give me any gage of thine, and I
will wear it in my bonnet: then, if ever thou
darest acknowledge it, I will make it my quarrel.

Will. Here's my glove: give me another of
thine.   230

K. Hen. There.

Will. This will I also wear in my cap: if ever
thou come to me and say after to-morrow, 'This
is my glove,' by this hand I will take thee a box
on the ear.

K. Hen. If ever I live to see it, I will challenge
it.   237

Will. Thou darest as well be hanged.

K. Hen. Well, I will do it, though I take thee
in the king's company.   240

Will. Keep thy word: fare thee well.

Bates. Be friends, you English fools, be
friends: we have French quarrels enow, if you
could tell how to reckon.   244

213 elder-gun: *popgun*   215 go about: *attempt*
219 round: *plain-spoken*   226 gage: *pledge*

K. Hen. Indeed, the French may lay twenty
French crowns to one, they will beat us; for
they bear them on their shoulders: but it is no
English treason to cut French crowns, and to-
morrow the king himself will be a clipper.   249

[*Exeunt Soldiers.*]

Upon the king! let us our lives, our souls,
Our debts, our careful wives,
Our children, and our sins lay on the king!   252
We must bear all. O hard condition!
Twin-born with greatness, subject to the breath
Of every fool, whose sense no more can feel
But his own wringing. What infinite heart's ease
Must kings neglect that private men enjoy!   257
And what have kings that privates have not too,
Save ceremony, save general ceremony?
And what art thou, thou idol ceremony?   260
What kind of god art thou, that suffer'st more
Of mortal griefs than do thy worshippers?
What are thy rents? what are thy comings-in?
O ceremony! show me but thy worth: 264
What is thy soul of adoration?
Art thou aught else but place, degree, and form,
Creating awe and fear in other men?
Wherein thou art less happy, being fear'd,   268
Than they in fearing.
What drink'st thou oft, instead of homage sweet,
But poison'd flattery? O! be sick, great greatness,
And bid thy ceremony give thee cure.   272
Think'st thou the fiery fever will go out
With titles blown from adulation?
Will it give place to flexure and low-bending?

246 French crowns; *cf. n.*   251 careful: *full of care*
256 wringing: *suffering*
265 *What is the essential reason men adore thee?*

Canst thou, when thou command'st the beggar's
    knee,   276
Command the health of it?   No, thou proud dream,
That play'st so subtly with a king's repose;
I am a king that find thee; and I know
'Tis not the balm, the sceptre and the ball,   280
The sword, the mace, the crown imperial,
The intertissued robe of gold and pearl,
The farced title running 'fore the king,
The throne he sits on, nor the tide of pomp   284
That beats upon the high shore of this world,
No, not all these, thrice-gorgeous ceremony,
Not all these, laid in bed majestical,
Can sleep so soundly as the wretched slave,   288
Who with a body fill'd and vacant mind
Gets him to rest, cramm'd with distressful bread;
Never sees horrid night, the child of hell,
But, like a lackey, from the rise to set   292
Sweats in the eye of Phœbus, and all night
Sleeps in Elysium; next day after dawn,
Doth rise and help Hyperion to his horse,
And follows so the ever-running year   296
With profitable labour to his grave:
And, but for ceremony, such a wretch,
Winding up days with toil and nights with sleep,
Had the fore-hand and vantage of a king.   300
The slave, a member of the country's peace,
Enjoys it; but in gross brain little wots
What watch the king keeps to maintain the peace,
Whose hours the peasant best advantages.   304

280 balm: *anointing oil* ·   ball: *carried by a king as a sign of sover-*
    eignty   282 intertissued: *interwoven*
283 farced: *stuffed out with pompous phrases; cf. n.*
290 distressful: *earned by painful labor*
295 help . . . horse: *is up before the sun*
300 Had: *would have*   fore-hand: *upper hand*   301 member: *sharer*
304 the peasant best advantages: *most benefit the peasant*

Enter Erpingham.

Erp. My lord, your nobles, jealous of your absence,
Seek through your camp to find you.
   K. Hen.   Good old knight,
Collect them all together at my tent:
I'll be before thee.
   Erp.   I shall do 't, my lord.   *Exit.*
   K. Hen. O God of battles! steel my soldiers'
      hearts;   309
Possess them not with fear; take from them now
The sense of reckoning, if the opposed numbers
Pluck their hearts from them. Not to-day, O
      Lord,   312
O, not to-day, think not upon the fault
My father made in compassing the crown!
I Richard's body have interr'd anew,
And on it have bestow'd more contrite tears   316
Than from it issu'd forced drops of blood.
Five hundred poor I have in yearly pay,
Who twice a day their wither'd hands hold up
Toward heaven, to pardon blood; and I have built   320
Two chantries, where the sad and solemn priests
Sing still for Richard's soul. More will I do;
Though all that I can do is nothing worth,
Since that my penitence comes after all,   324
Imploring pardon.

Enter Gloucester.

Glo. My liege!
K. Hen. My brother Gloucester's voice! Ay;

312 hearts: *courage*   314 compassing: *obtaining*
321 chantries; *cf. n.*   323-325 *Cf. n.*

I know thy errand, I will go with thee: 328
The day, my friends, and all things stay for me.
                                                    Exeunt.

Scene Two

[*The French Camp*]

Enter the Dauphin, Orleans, Rambures, and [*Others*].

Orl. The sun doth gild our armour: up, my lords!
Dau. Montez à cheval! My horse! varlet! lackey!
   ha!
Orl. O brave spirit!
Dau. Via! les eaux et la terre!   4
Orl. Rien puis? l'air et le feu.
Dau. Ciel! cousin Orleans.

Enter Constable.

Now, my lord constable!
   Con. Hark how our steeds for present service
    neigh!   8
   Dau. Mount them, and make incision in their hides,
That their hot blood may spin in English eyes,
And dout them with superfluous courage: ha!
   Ram. What! will you have them weep our horses'
    blood?   12
How shall we then behold their natural tears?

Enter Messenger.

Mess. The English are embattl'd, you French peers.
Con. To horse, you gallant princes! straight to
   horse!
Do but behold yon poor and starved band,   16
And your fair show shall suck away their souls,
Leaving them but the shales and husks of men.

4 Via: *away*   11 dout: *put out*   18 shales: *shells*

There is not work enough for all our hands;
Scarce blood enough in all their sickly veins   20
To give each naked curtal-axe a stain,
That our French gallants shall to-day draw out,
And sheathe for lack of sport: let us but blow on
      them,
The vapour of our valour will o'erturn them.   24
'Tis positive 'gainst all exceptions, lords,
That our superfluous lackeys and our peasants,
Who in unnecessary action swarm
About our squares of battle, were enow   28
To purge this field of such a hilding foe,
Though we upon this mountain's basis by
Took stand for idle speculation:
But that our honours must not. What's to say?
A very little little let us do,   33
And all is done. Then let the trumpets sound
The tucket sonance and the note to mount:
For our approach shall so much dare the field,
That England shall couch down in fear and yield.

Enter Grandpré.

  Grand. Why do you stay so long, my lords of
      France?
Yon island carrions desperate of their bones,
Ill-favour'dly become the morning field: 40
Their ragged curtains poorly are let loose,
And our air shakes them passing scornfully:
Big Mars seems bankrupt in their beggar'd host,
And faintly through a rusty beaver peeps: 44
The horsemen sit like fixed candlesticks,
With torch-staves in their hand; and their poor jades

21 curtal-axe: *long curved sword*   29 hilding: *base*
31 speculation: *looking-on*   35 tucket sonance: *preliminary notes*
36 dare; *cf. n.*   37 couch: *crouch*
41 curtains: *banners*   44 beaver: *visor of the helmet*

Lob down their heads, dropping the hides and hips,
The gum down-roping from their pale-dead eyes,   48
And in their pale dull mouths the gimmal'd bit
Lies foul with chew'd grass, still and motionless;
And their executors, the knavish crows,
Fly o'er them, all impatient for their hour.   52
Description cannot suit itself in words
To demonstrate the life of such a battle
In life so lifeless as it shows itself.

   Con. They have said their prayers, and they stay
     for death.   56
   Dau. Shall we go send them dinners and fresh
     suits,
And give their fasting horses provender,
And after fight with them?
   Con. I stay but for my guard: on, to the field!   60
I will the banner from a trumpet take,
And use it for my haste. Come, come, away!
The sun is high, and we outwear the day.   *Exeunt.*

Scene Three

[*The English Camp*]

*Enter Gloucester, Bedford, Exeter, Erpingham, with
   all his host: Salisbury, and Westmoreland.*

   Glo. Where is the king?
   Bed. The king himself is rode to view their battle.
   West. Of fighting men they have full three-score
     thousand.
   Exe. There's five to one; besides, they all are
     fresh.   4

47 Lob down: *droop*   48 down-roping: *hanging down*
49 gimmal'd: *made of rings or links*   60, 61 *Cf. n.*
61 trumpet: *trumpeter*   63 outwear: *are wasting*
2 battle: *battle lines*

Sal. God's arm strike with us! 'tis a fearful odds.
God be wi' you, princes all; I'll to my charge:
If we no more meet till we meet in heaven,
Then, joyfully, my noble Lord of Bedford,   8
My dear Lord Gloucester, and my good Lord Exeter,
And my kind kinsman, warriors all, adieu!

    Bed. Farewell, good Salisbury; and good luck go
      with thee!

    Exe. Farewell, kind lord. Fight valiantly to-
      day: 12
And yet I do thee wrong to mind thee of it,
For thou art fram'd of the firm truth of valour.

                             [*Exit Salisbury.*]

    Bed. He is as full of valour as of kindness;
Princely in both.

Enter the King.

    West.   O! that we now had here   16
But one ten thousand of those men in England
That do no work to-day.

    K. Hen.   What's he that wishes so?
My cousin Westmoreland? No, my fair cousin:
If we are mark'd to die, we are enow   20
To do our country loss; and if to live,
The fewer men, the greater share of honour.
God's will! I pray thee, wish not one man more.
By Jove, I am not covetous for gold,   24
Nor care I who doth feed upon my cost;
It yearns me not if men my garments wear;
Such outward things dwell not in my desires:
But if it be a sin to covet honour,   28
I am the most offending soul alive.
No, faith, my coz, wish not a man from England:

10 kinsman: *i.e., Westmoreland*   30 coz: *cousin*

God's peace! I would not lose so great an honour
As one man more, methinks, would share from me,   32
For the best hope I have. O! do not wish one more:
Rather proclaim it, Westmoreland, through my host,
That he which hath no stomach to this fight,
Let him depart; his passport shall be made,   36
And crowns for convoy put into his purse:
We would not die in that man's company
That fears his fellowship to die with us.
This day is call'd the feast of Crispian: 40
He that outlives this day, and comes safe home,
Will stand a tip-toe when this day is nam'd,
And rouse him at the name of Crispian.
He that shall live this day, and see old age,   44
Will yearly on the vigil feast his neighbours,
And say, 'To-morrow is Saint Crispian';
Then will he strip his sleeve and show his scars,
And say, 'These wounds I had on Crispin's day.'
Old men forget: yet all shall be forgot,   49
But he'll remember with advantages
What feats he did that day. Then shall our names,
Familiar in his mouth as household words,   52
Harry the king, Bedford and Exeter,
Warwick and Talbot, Salisbury and Gloucester,
Be in their flowing cups freshly remember'd.
This story shall the good man teach his son;   56
And Crispin Crispian shall ne'er go by,
From this day to the ending of the world,
But we in it shall be remembered;
We few, we happy few, we band of brothers;   60
For he to-day that sheds his blood with me
Shall be my brother; be he ne'er so vile,

37 convoy: *traveling expenses*   40 feast of Crispian: *October 25*
45 vigil: *eve of a feast-day*   50 advantages: *added details*
57 Crispin Crispian; *cf. n.*   62 vile: *low born*

This day shall gentle his condition:
And gentlemen in England, now a-bed,   64
Shall think themselves accurs'd they were not here,
And hold their manhoods cheap whiles any speaks
That fought with us upon Saint Crispin's day.

Enter Salisbury.

Sal. My sov'reign lord, bestow yourself with
    speed: 68
The French are bravely in their battles set,
And will with all expedience charge on us.

    K. Hen. All things are ready, if our minds be so.

    West. Perish the man whose mind is backward
    now!   72

    K. Hen. Thou dost not wish more help from Eng-
    land, coz?

    West. God's will! my liege, would you and I alone,
Without more help, could fight this royal battle!

    K. Hen. Why, now thou hast unwish'd five thou-
    sand men;   76
Which likes me better than to wish us one.
You know your places: God be with you all!

Tucket.   Enter Montjoy.

    Mont. Once more I come to know of thee, King
    Harry,
If for thy ransom thou wilt now compound,   80
Before thy most assured overthrow:
For certainly thou art so near the gulf
Thou needs must be englutted.   Besides, in mercy,
The constable desires thee thou wilt mind   84
Thy followers of repentance; that their souls

---

63 gentle his condition: *make him a gentleman*
68 bestow yourself: *take your post*
69 bravely: *with much display*   70 expedience: *speed*
80 compound: *come to terms*   83 englutted: *swallowed up*

May make a peaceful and a sweet retire
From off these fields, where, wretches, their poor
    bodies
Must lie and fester.
   K. Hen.   Who hath sent thee now?   88
   Mont. The Constable of France.
   K. Hen. I pray thee, bear my former answer back:
Bid them achieve me and then sell my bones.
Good God! why should they mock poor fellows
    thus?   92
The man that once did sell the lion's skin
While the beast liv'd, was kill'd with hunting him.
A many of our bodies shall no doubt
Find native graves; upon the which, I trust,   96
Shall witness live in brass of this day's work;
And those that leave their valiant bones in France,
Dying like men, though buried in your dung-hills,
They shall be fam'd; for there the sun shall greet
    them,   100
And draw their honours reeking up to heaven,
Leaving their earthly parts to choke your clime,
The smell whereof shall breed a plague in France.
Mark then abounding valour in our English,
That being dead, like to the bullet's grazing,   105
Break out into a second course of mischief,
Killing in relapse of mortality.
Let me speak proudly: tell the constable,   109
We are but warriors for the working-day;
Our gayness and our gilt are all besmirch'd
With rainy marching in the painful field;
There's not a piece of feather in our host—   112
Good argument, I hope, we will not fly—
And time hath worn us into slovenry:

91 achieve: *kill*   107 relapse of mortality: *a deadly rebound*
114 slovenry: *slovenliness*

But, by the mass, our hearts are in the trim;
And my poor soldiers tell me, yet ere night   116
They'll be in fresher robes, or they will pluck
The gay new coats o'er the French soldiers' heads,
And turn them out of service. If they do this,—
As, if God please, they shall,—my ransom then
Will soon be levied.   Herald, save thou thy
 labour;   121
Come thou no more for ransom, gentle herald:
They shall have none, I swear, but these my joints;
Which if they have as I will leave 'em them,   124
Shall yield them little, tell the constable.
 Mont. I shall, King Harry. And so, fare thee
  well:
Thou never shalt hear herald any more.   *Exit.*
 K. Hen. I fear thou'lt once more come again for
  ransom.   128

Enter York.

 York. My lord, most humbly on my knee I beg
The leading of the vaward.
 K. Hen. Take it, brave York. Now, soldiers,
  march away:
And how thou pleasest, God, dispose the day!

Exeunt.

Scene Four

[*The Field of Battle*]

Alarum: Excursions. Enter Pistol, French Soldier,
     [and] Boy.

 Pist. Yield, cur!
  Fr. Sol. Je pense que vous êtes gentilhomme de bonne qualité.

---

117 in fresher robes: *i.e., dead*   130 vaward: *vanguard*
Scene Four S. d. Excursions; *cf. n.*

Pist. Qualtitie calmie custure me.   Art thou a
gentleman?   4
What is thy name? discuss.

    Fr. Sol. O Seigneur Dieu!

    Pist. O Signieur Dew should be a gentleman:—
Perpend my words, O Signieur Dew, and mark:
O Signieur Dew, thou diest on point of fox   9
Except, O signieur, thou do give to me
Egregious ransom.

    Fr. Sol. O, prenez miséricorde! ayez pitié de
moi!   13

    Pist. Moy shall not serve; I will have forty moys;
Or I will fetch thy rim out at thy throat
In drops of crimson blood.   16

    Fr. Sol. Est-il impossible d'échapper la force
de ton bras?

    Pist. Brass, cur!
Thou damned and luxurious mountain goat,   20
Offer'st me brass?

    Fr. Sol. O pardonnez moi!

    Pist. Sayst thou me so? is that a ton of moys?
Come hither, boy: ask me this slave in French
What is his name.   25

    Boy. Écoutez: comment êtes-vous appelé?

    Fr. Sol. Monsieur le Fer.

    Boy. He says his name is Master Fer.   28

    Pist. Master Fer! I'll fer him, and firk him,
and ferret him.   Discuss the same in French
unto him.

    Boy. I do not know the French for fer, and
ferret, and firk.   33

---

4 Qualtitie calmie custure me; *cf. n.*   8 Perpend: *consider*
9 fox: *sword*   14 moys; *cf. n.*   15 rim: *midriff*
20 luxurious: *lustful*   29 firk: *beat*
30 ferret: *worry (as a ferret does its game)*

Pist. Bid him prepare, for I will cut his throat.

    Fr. Sol. Que dit-il, monsieur?   35

    Boy. Il me commande de vous dire que vous
faites vous prêt; car ce soldat ici est disposé
tout à cette heure de couper votre gorge.

Pist. Owy, cuppele gorge, permafoy,

Peasant,   unless   thou   give   me   crowns,   brave
    crowns;   40

Or mangled shalt thou be by this my sword.

    Fr. Sol. O! je vous supplie pour l'amour de
Dieu, me pardonner! Je suis gentilhomme de
bonne maison: gardez ma vie, et je vous don-
nerai deux cents écus.   45

Pist. What are his words?

    Boy. He prays you to save his life: he is a
gentleman of a good house; and for his ransom
he will give you two hundred crowns.   49

Pist. Tell him, my fury shall abate, and I
The crowns will take.

    Fr. Sol. Petit monsieur, que dit-il?   52

    Boy. Encore qu'il est contre son jurement
de pardonner aucun prisonnier; néanmoins,
pour les écus que vous l'avez promis, il est
content de vous donner la liberté, le franchise-
ment.   57

    Fr. Sol. Sur mes genoux, je vous donne mille
remercîments; et je m'estime heureux que je
suis tombé entre les mains d'un chevalier, je
pense, le plus brave, vaillant, et très distingué
seigneur d'Angleterre.

    Pist. Expound unto me, boy.   63

    Boy. He gives you, upon his knees, a thou-
sand thanks; and he esteems himself happy
that he hath fallen into the hands of one—as he

thinks—the most brave, valorous, and thrice-
worthy signieur of England.   68
Pist. As I suck blood, I will some mercy show.—
Follow me!

    Boy. Suivez-vous le grand capitaine. [*Exeunt
Pistol and French Soldier.*] I did never know so 72
full a voice issue from so empty a heart: but the
saying is true, 'The empty vessel makes the greatest sound.' Bardolph and Nym had ten times
more valour than this roaring devil i' the old play, 76
that every one may pare his nails with a wooden
dagger; and they are both hanged; and so would
this be if he durst steal anything adventurously.
I must stay with the lackeys, with the luggage 80
of our camp: the French might have a good
prey of us, if he knew of it; for there is none to
guard it but boys.   *Exit.*

Scene Five

[*Another Part of the Field*]

*Enter Constable, Orleans, Bourbon, Dauphin, and
Rambures.*

    Con. O diable!
    Orl. O seigneur! le jour est perdu! tout est perdu!
    Dau. Mort de ma vie! all is confounded, all!
Reproach and everlasting shame   4
Sit mocking in our plumes. O méchante fortune!
Do not run away.   *A short alarum.*
    Con.   Why, all our ranks are broke.
    Dau. O perdurable shame! let's stab ourselves.
Be these the wretches that we play'd at dice for?   8

76 devil i' the old play; *cf. n.*   7 perdurable: *everlasting*

Orl. Is this the king we sent to for his ransom?

Bour. Shame, and eternal shame, nothing but shame!

Let's die in honour! once more back again;
And he that will not follow Bourbon now,   12
Let him go hence, and with his cap in hand,
Like a base pander, hold the chamber-door
Whilst by a slave, no gentler than my dog,
His fairest daughter is contaminated.   16

Con. Disorder, that hath spoil'd us, friend us now!
Let us on heaps go offer up our lives.

Orl. We are enough yet living in the field
To smother up the English in our throngs,   20
If any order might be thought upon.

Bour. The devil take order now! I'll to the throng:
Let life be short, else shame will be too long.

                                Exit [with the others].

Scene Six

[*Another Part of the Field*]

*Alarum.   Enter the King and his train, with
                    Prisoners.*

K. Hen. Well have we done, thrice-valiant country-
          men:
But all's not done; yet keep the French the field.

Exe. The Duke of York commends him to your
          majesty.

K. Hen. Lives he, good uncle? thrice within this
          hour   4
I saw him down; thrice up again, and fighting;
From helmet to the spur all blood he was.

Exe. In which array, brave soldier, doth he lie,

18 on heaps: *in crowds*

Larding the plain; and by his bloody side,—   8
Yoke-fellow to his honour-owing wounds,—
The noble Earl of Suffolk also lies.
Suffolk first died: and York, all haggled over,
Comes to him, where in gore he lay insteep'd,   12
And takes him by the beard, kisses the gashes
That bloodily did yawn upon his face;
He cries aloud, "Tarry, my cousin Suffolk!
My soul shall thine keep company to heaven;   16
Tarry, sweet soul, for mine, then fly abreast,
As in this glorious and well-foughten field,
We kept together in our chivalry!"
Upon these words I came and cheer'd him up: 20
He smil'd me in the face, raught me his hand,
And with a feeble gripe says, 'Dear my lord,
Commend my service to my sovereign.'
So did he turn, and over Suffolk's neck   24
He threw his wounded arm, and kiss'd his lips;
And so espous'd to death, with blood he seal'd
A testament of noble-ending love.
The pretty and sweet manner of it forc'd   28
Those waters from me which I would have stopp'd;
But I had not so much of man in me,
And all my mother came into mine eyes
And gave me up to tears.
   K. Hen.   I blame you not;   32
For, hearing this, I must perforce compound
With mistful eyes, or they will issue too.   *Alarum.*
But hark! what new alarum is this same?
The French have reinforc'd their scatter'd men:
Then every soldier kill his prisoners!   37
Give the word through.   *Exit [with his train].*

8 Larding: *enriching (with his blood)*   9 honour-owing: *honorable*
11 haggled: *hacked*   21 raught: *reached*   34 issue: *shed tears*

S. presents the average man's (Fluella
opinion of
King Henry V

Scene Seven

[Another Part of the Field]

Enter Fluellen and Gower.

Flu. Kill the poys and the luggage! 'tis expressly against the law of arms: 'tis as arrant
a piece of knavery, mark you now, as can be
offer't: in your conscience now, is it not?   4

Gow. 'Tis certain, there's not a boy left alive;
and the cowardly rascals that ran from the
battle ha' done this slaughter: besides, they
have burned and carried away all that was in
the king's tent; wherefore the king most
worthily hath caused every soldier to cut his
prisoner's throat. O! 'tis a gallant king.   11

Flu. Ay, he was porn at Monmouth, Captain
Gower. What call you the town's name where
Alexander the Pig was born?

Gow. Alexander the Great.   15

Flu. Why, I pray you, is not pig great? The
pig, or the great, or the mighty, or the huge,
or the magnanimous, are all one reckonings,
save the phrase is a little variations.   19

Gow. I think Alexander the Great was born
in Macedon: his father was called Philip of
Macedon, as I take it.

Flu. I think it is in Macedon where Alexander is porn. I tell you, captain, if you look in
the maps of the 'orld, I warrant you sall find,
in the comparisons between Macedon and Monmouth, that the situations, look you, is both   27
alike. There is a river in Macedon, and there is
also moreover a river at Monmouth: it is called
Wye at Monmouth; but it is out of my prains

what is the name of the other river; but 'tis all
one, 'tis alike as my fingers is to my fingers, and
there is salmons in both. If you mark Alexander's life well, Harry of Monmouth's life is
come after it indifferent well; for there is figures 35
in all things. Alexander,—God knows, and you
know,—in his rages, and his furies, and his
wraths, and his cholers, and his moods, and his
displeasures, and his indignations, and also
being a little intoxicates in his prains, did, in
his ales and his angers, look you, kill his pest
friend, Cleitus.   42

   Gow. Our king is not like him in that: he
never killed any of his friends.

   Flu. It is not well done, mark you now, to
take the tales out of my mouth, ere it is made
and finished. I speak but in the figures and
comparisons of it: as Alexander killed his friend 48
Cleitus, being in his ales and his cups, so also
Harry Monmouth, being in his right wits and
his good judgments, turned away the fat knight
with the great belly-doublet: he was full of
jests, and gipes, and knaveries, and mocks; I
have forgot his name.   54

   Gow. Sir John Falstaff.

   Flu. That is he. I'll tell you, there is goot
men porn at Monmouth.

   Gow. Here comes his majesty.   58

*Alarum.   Enter King Harry and Bourbon with
   [other] prisoners [Warwick, Gloucester, Exeter,
   and Others]. Flourish.*

   K. Hen. I was not angry since I came to France

34, 35 is come after: *resembles*   35 figures: *analogues*
53 gipes: *jokes*

Until this instant.   Take a trumpet, herald;   60
Ride thou unto the horsemen on yon hill:
If they will fight with us, bid them come down,
Or void the field; they do offend our sight.
If they'll do neither, we will come to them,   64
And make them skirr away, as swift as stones
Enforced from the old Assyrian slings.
Besides, we'll cut the throats of those we have,
And not a man of them that we shall take   68
Shall taste our mercy.   Go and tell them so.

Enter Montjoy.

Exe. Here comes the herald of the French, my
    liege.
Glo. His eyes are humbler than they us'd to be.
K. Hen. How now! what means this, herald?
    know'st thou not   72
That I have fin'd these bones of mine for ransom?
Com'st thou again for ransom?
    Mont.   No, great king.
I come to thee for charitable licence,
That we may wander o'er this bloody field   76
To book our dead, and then to bury them;
To sort our nobles from our common men;
For many of our princes—woe the while!—
Lie drown'd and soak'd in mercenary blood;   80
So do our vulgar drench their peasant limbs
In blood of princes; and their wounded steeds
Fret fetlock-deep in gore, and with wild rage
Yerk out their armed heels at their dead masters,   84
Killing them twice.   O! give us leave, great king,
To view the field in safety and dispose

63 void: *leave*   65 skirr: *scurry*
73 fin'd: *fixed as the price to be paid*   77 book: *record*
81 vulgar: *common soldiers*   84 Yerk: *strike*

Of their dead bodies.

   K. Hen.   I tell thee truly, herald,

I know not if the day be ours or no;   88

For yet a many of your horsemen peer

And gallop o'er the field.

   Mont.   The day is yours.

   K. Hen. Praised be God, and not our strength,
   for it!

What is this castle call'd that stands hard by?

   Mont. They call it Agincourt.   93

   K. Hen. Then call we this the field of Agincourt,

Fought on the day of Crispin Crispianus.

   Flu. Your grandfather of famous memory,
an 't please your majesty, and your great-uncle
Edward the Plack Prince of Wales, as I have
read in the chronicles, fought a most prave
pattle here in France.   100

   K. Hen. They did, Fluellen.

   Flu. Your majesty says very true. If your
majesties is remembered of it, the Welshmen
did good service in a garden where leeks did
grow, wearing leeks in their Monmouth caps;
which, your majesty know, to this hour is an
honourable badge of the service; and I do believe, your majesty takes no scorn to wear the
leek upon Saint Tavy's day.   109

   K. Hen. I wear it for a memorable honour;

For I am Welsh, you know, good countryman.

   Flu. All the water in Wye cannot wash your
majesty's Welsh plood out of your pody, I can
tell you that: Got pless it and preserve it, as long
as it pleases his grace, and his majesty too!

---

89 peer: *appear*   96 grandfather: *i.e., great-grandfather*
104 in a garden; *cf. n.*   105 Monmouth caps; *cf n.*
109 Tavy's: *David's*

K. Hen. Thanks, good my countryman.   116

Flu. By Jeshu, I am your majesty's countryman, I care not who know it; I will confess it to
all the 'orld: I need not be ashamed of your
majesty, praised be God, so long as your majesty
is an honest man.   121

K. Hen. God keep me so!   *Enter Williams.*
                              Our heralds go with him:
Bring me just notice of the numbers dead
On both our parts.   Call yonder fellow hither.

                  [*Exeunt Heralds with Montjoy.*]

Exe. Soldier, you must come to the king.

K. Hen. Soldier, why wear'st thou that glove in
thy cap?   127

Will. An 't please your majesty, 'tis the gage
of one that I should fight withal, if he be alive.

K. Hen. An Englishman?

Will. An 't please your majesty, a rascal that
swaggered with me last night; who, if a' live and
ever dare to challenge this glove, I have sworn to
take him a box o' the ear: or, if I can see my
glove in his cap,—which he swore as he was a
soldier he would wear if alive,—I will strike it
out soundly.   137

K. Hen. What think you, Captain Fluellen?
is it fit this soldier keep his oath?

Flu. He is a craven and a villain else, an 't
please your majesty, in my conscience.   141

K. Hen. It may be his enemy is a gentleman
of great sort, quite from the answer of his degree.

Flu. Though he be as good a gentleman as
the devil is, as Lucifer and Belzebub himself, it

---

123 just notice: *exact information*   124 parts: *sides*
143 great sort: *high rank*   from . . . degree: *above answering the*
    challenge of one of his rank

is necessary, look your Grace, that he keep his
vow and his oath.   If he be perjured, see you
now, his reputation is as arrant a villain and a
Jack-sauce as ever his black shoe trod upon
God's ground and his earth, in my conscience,
la!   151

K. Hen. Then keep thy vow, sirrah, when
thou meetest the fellow.

Will. So I will, my liege, as I live.

K. Hen. Who servest thou under?

Will. Under Captain Gower, my liege.   156

Flu. Gower is a goot captain, and is good
knowledge and literatured in the wars.

K. Hen. Call him hither to me, soldier.

Will. I will, my liege.   *Exit.*

K. Hen. Here, Fluellen; wear thou this favour
for me and stick it in thy cap.   When Alençon 162
and myself were down together I plucked this
glove from his helm: if any man challenge this,
he is a friend to Alençon, and an enemy to our
person; if thou encounter any such, apprehend
him, and thou dost me love.   167

Flu. Your Grace does me as great honours as
can be desired in the hearts of his subjects: I
would fain see the man that has but two legs
that shall find himself aggriefed at this glove,
that is all; but I would fain see it once, and
please God of his grace that I might see.   173

K. Hen. Knowest thou Gower?

Flu. He is my dear friend, an 't please you.

K. Hen. Pray thee, go seek him, and bring
him to my tent.   177

Flu. I will fetch him.   *Exit.*

149 Jack-sauce: *impudent rascal*   167 love: *an act of kindness*

    K. Hen. My Lord of Warwick, and my brother
      Gloucester,
Follow Fluellen closely at the heels.   180
The glove which I have given him for a favour
May haply purchase him a box o' the ear;
It is the soldier's; I by bargain should
Wear it myself. Follow, good cousin Warwick:
If that the soldier strike him,—as I judge   185
By his blunt bearing he will keep his word,—
Some sudden mischief may arise of it;
For I do know Fluellen valiant,   188
And touch'd with choler, hot as gunpowder,
And quickly will return an injury:
Follow and see there be no harm between them.
Go you with me, uncle of Exeter.   *Exeunt.*

Scene Eight

[Before King Henry's Pavilion]

Enter Gower and Williams.

    Will. I warrant it is to knight you, captain.

Enter Fluellen.

    Flu. God's will and his pleasure, captain, I
peseech you now come apace to the king: there
is more good toward you peradventure than is
in your knowledge to dream of.   5
    Will. Sir, know you this glove?
    Flu. Know the glove! I know the glove is a glove.
    Will. I know this; and thus I challenge it.   8
                          Strikes him.
    Flu. 'Sblood! an arrant traitor as any's in
the universal world, or in France, or in England.

4 toward: *intended for*   9 'Sblood: *God's blood*

Gow. How now, sir ! you villain !

Will. Do you think I'll be forsworn?   12

Flu. Stand away, Captain Gower; I will give treason his payment into plows, I warrant you.

Will. I am no traitor.

Flu. That's a lie in thy throat. I charge you in his majesty's name, apprehend him: he is a friend of the Duke Alençon's.   18

Enter Warwick and Gloucester.

War. How now, how now ! what's the matter?

Flu. My Lord of Warwick, here is,—praised be God for it !—a most contagious treason come to light, look you, as you shall desire in a summer's day. Here is his majesty.

Enter King and Exeter.

K. Hen. How now ! what's the matter?   24

Flu. My liege, here is a villain and a traitor, that, look your Grace, has struck the glove which your majesty is take out of the helmet of Alençon.

Will. My liege, this was my glove; here is the fellow of it; and he that I gave it to in change promised to wear it in his cap: I promised to strike him, if he did: I met this man with my glove in his cap, and I have been as good as my word.   28   33

Flu. Your majesty hear now,—saving your majesty's manhood,—what an arrant, rascally, beggarly, lousy knave it is. I hope your majesty is pear me testimony and witness, and will avouchment, that this is the glove of Alençon that your majesty is give me; in your conscience now.

---

37 is pear: *will bear*   38 avouchment: *make acknowledgment*

K. Hen. Give me thy glove, soldier: look,
here is the fellow of it.   41
'Twas I, indeed, thou promisedst to strike;
And thou hast given me most bitter terms.

Flu. An 't please your majesty, let his neck
answer for it, if there is any martial law in the
'orld.

K. Hen. How canst thou make me satis-
faction?   48

Will. All offences, my lord, come from the
heart: never came any from mine that might
offend your majesty.

K. Hen. It was ourself thou didst abuse.

Will. Your majesty came not like yourself:
you appeared to me but as a common man;
witness the night, your garments, your lowliness; and what your highness suffered under 56
that shape, I beseech you, take it for your own
fault and not mine: for had you been as I took
you for, I made no offence; therefore, I beseech
your highness, pardon me.   60

K. Hen. Here, uncle Exeter, fill this glove with
   crowns,
And give it to this fellow. Keep it, fellow;
And wear it for an honour in thy cap
Till I do challenge it. Give him the crowns: 64
And, captain, you must needs be friends with him.

Flu. By this day and this light, the fellow
has mettle enough in his belly. Hold, there is
twelve pence for you, and I pray you to serve 68
God, and keep you out of prawls, and prabbles,
and quarrels, and dissensions, and, I warrant
you, it is the better for you.

43 terms: *words*   55 lowliness: *humble bearing*
69 prabbles: *squabbles*

Will. I will none of your money.   72

Flu. It is with a good will; I can tell you it
will serve you to mend your shoes: come, wherefore should you be so pashful? your shoes is not
so good: 'tis a good shilling, I warrant you, or I
will change it.   77

Enter [an English] Herald.

K. Hen. Now, herald, are the dead number'd?

Her. Here is the number of the slaughter'd French.

K. Hen. What prisoners of good sort are taken,
    uncle?   80

Exe. Charles Duke of Orleans, nephew to the king;
John Duke of Bourbon, and Lord Bouciqualt:
Of other lords and barons, knights and squires,
Full fifteen hundred, besides common men.   84

K. Hen. This note doth tell me of ten thousand
    French
That in the field lie slain: of princes, in this number,
And nobles bearing banners, there lie dead
One hundred twenty-six: added to these,   88
Of knights, esquires, and gallant gentlemen,
Eight thousand and four hundred; of the which
Five hundred were but yesterday dubb'd knights:
So that, in these ten thousand they have lost,   92
There are but sixteen hundred mercenaries;
The rest are princes, barons, lords, knights, squires,
And gentlemen of blood and quality.
The names of those their nobles that lie dead: 96
Charles Delabreth, High Constable of France;
Jaques of Chatillon, Admiral of France;
The master of the cross-bows, Lord Rambures;

80 good sort: *rank*

Battle of Agincourt was
miraculous victory for Eng.
102   The Life of

Great Master of France, the brave Sir Guichard
    Dolphin;   100
John Duke of Alençon; Anthony Duke of Brabant,
The brother to the Duke of Burgundy,
And Edward Duke of Bar: of lusty earls,
Grandpré and Roussi, Fauconberg and Foix,   104
Beaumont and Marle, Vaudemont and Lestrale.
Here was a royal fellowship of death!
Where is the number of our English dead?
               [*Herald presents another paper.*]
Edward the Duke of York, the Earl of Suffolk,
Sir Richard Ketly, Davy Gam, esquire: 109
None else of name: and of all other men
But five and twenty. O God! thy arm was here;
And not to us, but to thy arm alone,   112
Ascribe we all. When, without stratagem,
But in plain shock and even play of battle,
Was ever known so great and little loss
On one part and on the other? Take it, God,
For it is none but thine!
    Exe.   'Tis wonderful!   117
    K. Hen. Come, go we in procession to the village:
And be it death proclaimed through our host
To boast of this or take the praise from God   120
Which is his only.
    Flu. Is it not lawful, an please your majesty,
    to tell how many is killed?
    K. Hen. Yes, captain; but with this acknowledg-
    ment,   124
That God fought for us.
    Flu. Yes, my conscience, he did us great good.
    K. Hen. Do we all holy rites:
Let there be sung 'Non nobis' and 'Te Deum';   128

---

110 name: *eminence*

The dead with charity enclos'd in clay.
And then to Calais; and to England then,
Where ne'er from France arriv'd more happy men.

Exeunt.

ACT FIVE

Enter Chorus.

Vouchsafe to those that have not read the story,
That I may prompt them: and of such as have,
I humbly pray them to admit the excuse
Of time, of numbers, and due course of things, **4**
Which cannot in their huge and proper life
Be here presented.   Now we bear the king
Toward Calais: grant him there; there seen,
Heave him away upon your winged thoughts **8**
Athwart the sea.   Behold, the English beach
Pales in the flood with men, with wives, and boys,
Whose shouts and claps out-voice the deep-mouth'd
    sea,
Which, like a mighty whiffler 'fore the king, **12**
Seems to prepare his way: so let him land
And solemnly see him set on to London.
So swift a pace hath thought that even now
You may imagine him upon Blackheath; **16**
Where that his lords desire him to have borne
His bruised helmet and his bended sword
Before him through the city: he forbids it,
Being free from vainness and self-glorious pride; **20**
Giving full trophy, signal and ostent,
Quite from himself, to God.   But now behold,
In the quick forge and working-house of thought,

7 grant: *imagine*   10 Pales in: *encompasses*
12 whiffler: *officer who went at the head of a procession*
21 signal: *symbols of victory*   ostent: *triumphal show*

How London doth pour out her citizens.   24
The mayor and all his brethren in best sort,
Like to the senators of the antique Rome,
With the plebeians swarming at their heels,
Go forth and fetch their conquering Cæsar in:
As, by a lower but loving likelihood,   29
Were now the general of our gracious empress,—
As in good time he may,—from Ireland coming,
Bringing rebellion broached on his sword,   32
How many would the peaceful city quit
To welcome him! much more, and much more cause,
Did they this Harry. Now in London place him;
As yet the lamentation of the French   36
Invites the King of England's stay at home,—
The emperor's coming in behalf of France,
To order peace between them;—and omit
All the occurrences, whatever chanc'd,   40
Till Harry's back-return again to France:
There must we bring him; and myself have play'd
The interim, by remembering you 'tis past.
Then brook abridgment, and your eyes advance,
After your thoughts, straight back again to France.
                                                    Exit.

Scene One

[France.   The English camp]

Enter Fluellen and Gower.

Gow. Nay, that's right; but why wear you
your leek to-day? Saint Davy's day is past.
Flu. There is occasions and causes why and
wherefore in all things: I will tell you, asse my 4
friend, Captain Gower. The rascally, scald,

25 sort: *array*   30 general: *Earl of Essex; cf. n.*
32 broached: *transfixed*   38 emperor's; *cf. n.*
39 order: *arrange*   5 scald: *scurvy*

beggarly, lousy, pragging knave, Pistol,—which
you and yourself and all the world know to be no
petter than a fellow, look you now, of no merits,— 8
he is come to me and prings me pread and salt
yesterday, look you, and pid me eat my leek. It
was in a place where I could not preed no contention with him; but I will be so pold as to 12
wear it in my cap till I see him once again, and
then I will tell him a little piece of my desires.

Gow. Why, here he comes, swelling like a
turkey-cock.   16

Enter Pistol.

Flu. 'Tis no matter for his swellings nor his
turkey-cocks. God pless you, Aunchient Pistol!
you scurvy, lousy knave, God pless you!
Pist. Ha! art thou bedlam? dost thou thirst, base
    Troyan,   20
To have me fold up Parca's fatal web?
Hence! I am qualmish at the smell of leek.

Flu. I peseech you heartily, scurvy, lousy
knave, at my desires and my requests and my 24
petitions to eat, look you, this leek; pecause,
look you, you do not love it, nor your affections
and your appetites and your digestions does not
agree with it, I would desire you to eat it.   28

Pist. Not for Cadwallader and all his goats.

Flu. There is one goat for you. *Strikes him.*
Will you be so good, scald knave, as eat it?

Pist. Base Troyan, thou shalt die.   32

Flu. You say very true, scald knave, when
God's will is. I will desire you to live in the

11, 12 preed . . . contention: *push a quarrel*
20 bedlam: *mad*   Troyan: *Trojan, cant term for rioter*
21 Parca: *i.e., Parcæ, the Fates*
29 Cadwallader: *the last of the Welsh kings*

mean time and eat your victuals; come, there
is sauce for it. [*Strikes him again.*] You called 36
me yesterday mountain-squire, but I will make
you to-day a squire of low degree. I pray you, fall
to: if you can mock a leek, you can eat a leek.

Gow. Enough, captain: you have astonished
him.   41

Flu. I say, I will make him eat some part of
my leek, or I will peat his pate four days. Bite,
I pray you; it is good for your green wound and
your ploody coxcomb.   45

Pist. Must I bite?

Flu. Yes, certainly, and out of doubt and
out of question too and ambiguities.   48

Pist. By this leek, I will most horribly revenge. I eat and eat, I swear—

Flu. Eat, I pray you: will you have some
more sauce to your leek? there is not enough
leek to swear by.   53

Pist. Quiet thy cudgel: thou dost see I eat.

Flu. Much good do you, scald knave, heartily. Nay, pray you, throw none away; the
skin is good for your broken coxcomb. When
you take occasions to see leeks hereafter, I pray
you, mock at 'em; that is all.

Pist. Good.   60

Flu. Ay, leeks is good. Hold you, there is a
groat to heal your pate.

Pist. Me a groat!

Flu. Yes, verily and in truth, you shall take
it; or I have another leek in my pocket, which
you shall eat.   66

40 astonished: *stunned (?)*   45 coxcomb: *head*
62 groat: *a coin worth fourpence*

Pist. I take thy groat in earnest of revenge.

Flu. If I owe you anything I will pay you in
cudgels: you shall be a woodmonger, and buy
nothing of me but cudgels. God be wi' you, and
keep you, and heal your pate.   *Exit.*

Pist. All hell shall stir for this.   72

Gow. Go, go; you are a countcrfcit cowardly
knave. Will you mock at an ancient tradition,
begun upon an honourable respect, and worn as
a memorable trophy of predeceased valour, and 76
dare not avouch in your deeds any of your words?
I have seen you gleeking and galling at this
gentleman twice or thrice. You thought, because he could not speak English in the native 80
garb, he could not therefore handle an English
cudgel: you find it otherwise; and henceforth
let a Welsh correction teach you a good English
condition. Fare ye well.   *Exit.*

Pist. Doth Fortune play the huswife with me
   now?   85
News have I that my Doll is dead i' the spital
Of malady of France:
And there my rendezvous is quite cut off.   88
Old I do wax, and from my weary limbs
Honour is cudgell'd. Well, bawd I'll turn,
And something lean to cutpurse of quick hand.
To England will I steal, and there I'll steal: 92
And patches will I get unto these cudgell'd scars,
And swear I got them in the Gallia wars.   *Exit.*

75 respect: *consideration*   77 avouch: *support*
78 gleeking: *scoffing*   galling: *jeering*   81 garb: *manner*
84 condition: *disposition*   85 huswife: *jilt*

Scene Two

[An Apartment in the French King's Palace]

Enter at one door, King Henry, Exeter, Bedford,
Warwick, [Gloucester, Clarence,] and other
Lords; at another, Queen Isabel, [the Princess
Katharine, Alice and other Ladies,] the [French]
King, the Duke of Burgundy, and other French.

   K. Hen. Peace to this meeting, wherefore we are
   met!
Unto our brother France, and to our sister,
Health and fair time of day; joy and good wishes
To our most fair and princely cousin Katharine;
And, as a branch and member of this royalty,   5
By whom this great assembly is contriv'd,
We do salute you, Duke of Burgundy;
And, princes French, and peers, health to you all! 8
   Fr. King. Right joyous are we to behold your face,
Most worthy brother England; fairly met:
So are you, princes English, every one.
   Q. Isa. So happy be the issue, brother England,
Of this good day and of this gracious meeting,   13
As we are now glad to behold your eyes;
Your eyes, which hitherto have borne in them
Against the French, that met them in their bent,
The fatal balls of murdering basilisks: 17
The venom of such looks, we fairly hope,
Have lost their quality, and that this day
Shall change all griefs and quarrels into love.   20
   K. Hen. To cry amen to that, thus we appear.
   Q. Isa. You English princes all, I do salute you.
   Bur. My duty to you both, on equal love,

---

3 fair time of day: *a common form of greeting*
16 bent: *aim or glance*   17 basilisks: *large cannon; cf. n.*

Great Kings of France and England! That I have
    labour'd   24
With all my wits, my pains, and strong endeavours,
To bring your most imperial majesties
Unto this bar and royal interview,
Your mightiness on both parts best can witness.
Since then my office hath so far prevail'd   29
That face to face, and royal eye to eye,
You have congreeted, let it not disgrace me
If I demand before this royal view,   32
What rub or what impediment there is,
Why that the naked, poor, and mangled Peace,
Dear nurse of arts, plenties, and joyful births,
Should not in this best garden of the world,   36
Our fertile France, put up her lovely visage?
Alas! she hath from France too long been chas'd,
And all her husbandry doth lie on heaps,
Corrupting in it own fertility.   40
Her vine, the merry cheerer of the heart,
Unpruned dies; her hedges even-pleach'd,
Like prisoners wildly overgrown with hair,
Put forth disorder'd twigs; her fallow leas   44
The darnel, hemlock and rank fumitory
Doth root upon, while that the coulter rusts
That should deracinate such savagery;
The even mead, that erst brought sweetly forth   48
The freckled cowslip, burnet, and green clover,
Wanting the scythe, all uncorrected, rank,
Conceives by idleness, and nothing teems
But hateful docks, rough thistles, kecksies, burs,

27 bar: *barrier; place of meeting*
31 congreeted: *exchanged greetings*
42 even-pleach'd: *evenly interwoven*
45 darnel: *a weed injurious to crops*
    taste
47 deracinate: *uproot*

32 view: *presence*   40 it: *its*
            44 leas: *arable land*
fumitory: *a weed with a bitter*
        46 coulter: *ploughshare*
        52 kecksies: *dry stalks*

Losing both beauty and utility;   53
And all our vineyards, fallows, meads, and hedges,
Defective in their natures, grow to wildness.
Even so our houses and ourselves and children
Have lost, or do not learn for want of time,   57
The sciences that should become our country,
But grow like savages,—as soldiers will,
That nothing do but meditate on blood,—   60
To swearing and stern looks, diffus'd attire,
And everything that seems unnatural.
Which to reduce into our former favour
You are assembled; and my speech entreats   64
That I may know the let why gentle Peace
Should not expel these inconveniences,
And bless us with her former qualities.

    K. Hen. If, Duke of Burgundy, you would the
      peace,   68
Whose want gives growth to the imperfections
Which you have cited, you must buy that peace
With full accord to all our just demands;
Whose tenours and particular effects   72
You have, enschedul'd briefly, in your hands.

    Bur. The king hath heard them; to the which as
      yet,
There is no answer made.

    K. Hen.   Well then the peace,
Which you before so urg'd, lies in his answer.   76

    Fr. King. I have but with a cursorary eye
O'erglanc'd the articles: pleaseth your Grace
To appoint some of your council presently
To sit with us once more, with better heed   80

---

61 diffus'd: *disordered*   63 reduce: *bring back*   favour: *aspect*
65 let: *impediment*   72 tenours: *purport*
73 enschedul'd: *drawn up in writing*   77 cursorary: *cursory*

To re-survey them, we will suddenly
Pass our accept and peremptory answer.

    K. Hen. Brother, we shall. Go, uncle Exeter,
And brother Clarence, and you, brother Gloucester, 84
Warwick and Huntingdon, go with the king;
And take with you free power to ratify,
Augment, or alter, as your wisdoms best
Shall see advantageable for our dignity,   88
Anything in or out of our demands,
And we'll consign thereto. Will you, fair sister,
Go with the princes, or stay here with us?

    Q. Isa. Our gracious brother, I will go with
    them.   92
Haply a woman's voice may do some good
When articles too nicely urg'd be stood on.

    K. Hen. Yet leave our cousin Katharine here with
    us:
She is our capital demand, compris'd   96
Within the fore-rank of our articles.

    Q. Isa. She hath good leave.
           Exeunt [all except King Henry, Katharine,
                          and Alice].

    K. Hen.   Fair Katharine, and most fair!
Will you vouchsafe to teach a soldier terms,
Such as will enter at a lady's ear,   100
And plead his love-suit to her gentle heart?

    Kath. Your majesty shall mock at me; I can-
not speak your England.

    K. Hen. O fair Katharine! if you will love
me soundly with your French heart, I will be
glad to hear you confess it brokenly with your
English tongue. Do you like me, Kate?   107

81 suddenly: *soon*   82 accept: *decisive*   peremptory: *final*
90 consign: *agree*   96 capital: *chief*

Kath. Pardonnez-moi, I cannot tell wat is 'like me.'

K. Hen. An angel is like you, Kate; and you are like an angel.

Kath. Que dit-il? que je suis semblable à les anges?   113

Alice. Oui, vraiment, sauf votre grace, ainsi dit-il.

K. Hen. I said so, dear Katharine; and I must not blush to affirm it.   117

Kath. O bon Dieu! les langues des hommes sont pleines de tromperies.

K. Hen. What says she, fair one? that the tongues of men are full of deceits?   121

Alice. Oui, dat de tongues of de mans is be full of deceits: dat is de princess.

K. Hen. The princess is the better English-woman. I' faith, Kate, my wooing is fit for thy understanding: I am glad thou canst speak no better English; for, if thou couldst, thou wouldst find me such a plain king that thou wouldst think I had sold my farm to buy my crown. I 129 know no ways to mince it in love, but directly to say 'I love you': then, if you urge me further than to say 'Do you in faith?' I wear out my suit. Give me your answer; i' faith do: and so clap hands and a bargain. How say you, lady?

Kath. Sauf votre honneur, me understand well.

K. Hen. Marry, if you would put me to verses, or to dance for your sake, Kate, why you undid 137 me: for the one, I have neither words nor measure, and for the other, I have no strength in measure, yet a reasonable measure in strength.

137 undid: *would undo*   138 measure; *cf. n.*

If I could win a lady at leap-frog, or by vaulting
into my saddle with my armour on my back,
under the correction of bragging be it spoken,
I should quickly leap into a wife. Or if I might
buffet for my love, or bound my horse for her 145
favours, I could lay on like a butcher and sit
like a jack-an-apes, never off. But before God,
Kate, I cannot look greenly nor gasp out my
eloquence, nor I have no cunning in protesta-
tion; only downright oaths, which I never use
till urged, nor never break for urging. If thou
canst love a fellow of this temper, Kate, whose
face is not worth sun-burning, that never looks 153
in his glass for love of anything he sees there,
let thine eye be thy cook. I speak to thee plain
soldier: if thou canst love me for this, take me;
if not, to say to thee that I shall die, is true; but
for thy love, by the Lord, no; yet I love thee
too. And while thou livest, dear Kate, take a
fellow of plain and uncoined constancy, for he
perforce must do thee right, because he hath 161
not the gift to woo in other places; for these
fellows of infinite tongue, that can rime themselves into ladies' favours, they do always reason
themselves out again. What! a speaker is but
a prater; a rime is but a ballad. A good leg
will fall, a straight back will stoop, a black beard
will turn white, a curled pate will grow bald, a
fair face will wither, a full eye will wax hollow, 169
but a good heart, Kate, is the sun and the
moon; or, rather, the sun, and not the moon;

145 buffet: *box*   bound my horse: *make my horse leap*
147 jack-an-apes: *monkey*   148 greenly: *foolishly*
149 cunning: *skill*   152 temper: *disposition*
155 let . . . cook; *cf. n.*   160 uncoined constancy; *cf. n.*
167 fall: *shrink*

for it shines bright and never changes, but keeps
his course truly. If thou would have such a one,
take me; and take me, take a soldier; take a
soldier, take a king. And what sayest thou then to
my love? speak, my fair, and fairly, I pray thee.

Kath. Is it possible dat I sould love de
enemy of France?   178

K. Hen. No; it is not possible you should
love the enemy of France, Kate; but, in loving
me, you should love the friend of France; for
I love France so well, that I will not part with
a village of it; I will have it all mine: and,
Kate, when France is mine and I am yours,
then yours is France and you are mine.   185

Kath. I cannot tell wat is dat.

K. Hen. No, Kate? I will tell thee in French,
which I am sure will hang upon my tongue like
a new-married wife about her husband's neck,
hardly to be shook off. Je quand sur le possession de France, et quand vous avez le possession
de moi,—let me see, what then? Saint Denis 192
be my speed!—donc votre est France, et vous
êtes mienne. It is as easy for me, Kate, to
conquer the kingdom, as to speak so much
more French: I shall never move thee in French,
unless it be to laugh at me.   197

Kath. Sauf votre honneur, le français que
vous parlez, il est meilleur que l'anglais lequel je
parle.   200

K. Hen. No, faith, is 't not, Kate; but thy
speaking of my tongue, and I thine, most truly
falsely, must needs be granted to be much at

192 Saint Denis: *patron saint of France*
193 be my speed: *aid me*

one.   But, Kate, dost thou understand thus
much English, Canst thou love me?   205

Kath. I cannot tell.

K. Hen. Can any of your neighbours tell,
Kate? I'll ask them. Come, I know thou lovest
me; and at night when you come into your
closet you'll question this gentlewoman about 210
me; and I know, Kate, you will to her dispraise
those parts in me that you love with your heart:
but, good Kate, mock me mercifully; the rather,
gentle princess, because I love thee cruelly. If
ever thou be'st mine, Kate,—as I have a saving
faith within me tells me thou shalt,—I get thee
with scambling, and thou must therefore needs 217
prove a good soldier-breeder. Shall not thou
and I, between Saint Denis and Saint George,
compound a boy, half French, half English,
that shall go to Constantinople and take the
Turk by the beard? shall we not? what sayest
thou, my fair flower-de-luce?

Kath. I do not know dat.   224

K. Hen. No; 'tis hereafter to know, but now
to promise: do but now promise, Kate, you will
endeavour for your French part of such a boy,
and for my English moiety take the word of a
king and a bachelor. How answer you, la plus
belle Katharine du monde, mon très cher et
devin déesse?   231

Kath. Your majesté ave fausse French enough
to deceive de most sage demoiselle dat is en
France.   234

K. Hen. Now, fie upon my false French! By

203, 204 at one: *alike*   210 closet: *chamber*   217 scambling: *fighting*
223 flower-de-luce: *fleur-de-lys, the emblem of France*
228 moiety: *half*

mine honour, in true English I love thee, Kate:
by which honour I dare not swear thou lovest
me; yet my blood begins to flatter me that thou
dost, notwithstanding the poor and untempering
effect of my visage. Now beshrew my father's 240
ambition! he was thinking of civil wars when
he got me: therefore was I created with a stub-
born outside, with an aspect of iron, that, when
I come to woo ladies, I fright them. But, in
faith, Kate, the elder I wax the better I shall
appear: my comfort is, that old age, that ill
layer-up of beauty, can do no more spoil upon
my face: thou hast me, if thou hast me, at the 248
worst; and thou shalt wear me, if thou wear me,
better and better. And therefore tell me, most
fair Katharine, will you have me? Put off your
maiden blushes; avouch the thoughts of your
heart with the looks of an empress; take me
by the hand, and say 'Harry of England, I am
thine': which word thou shalt no sooner bless
mine ear withal, but I will tell thee aloud, 256
'England is thine, Ireland is thine, France is
thine, and Henry Plantagenet is thine'; who,
though I speak it before his face, if he be not
fellow with the best king, thou shalt find the 260
best king of good fellows. Come, your answer
in broken music; for thy voice is music, and
thy English broken; therefore, queen of all,
Katharine, break thy mind to me in broken
English: wilt thou have me?   265

    Kath. Dat is as it shall please de roi mon père.

.139 untempering: *unsoftening*   240 beshrew: *a plague upon*
247 layer-up: *preserver*   260 fellow with: *a match for*
262 broken music; *cf. n.*   264 break: *disclose*

K. Hen. Nay, it will please him well, Kate;
it shall please him, Kate.   268

Kath. Den it shall also content me.

K. Hen. Upon that I kiss your hand, and I
call you my queen.

Kath. Laissez, mon seigneur, laissez, laissez!
Ma foi, je ne veux point que vous abaissiez votre
grandeur, en baisant la main d'une de votre seig-
neurie indigne serviteur: excusez-moi, je vous
supplie, mon très-puissant seigneur.   276

K. Hen. Then I will kiss your lips, Kate.

Kath. Les dames, et demoiselles, pour être
baisées devant leur noces, il n'est pas la cou-
tume de France.   280

K. Hen. Madam my interpreter, what says she?

Alice. Dat it is not be de fashion pour les
ladies of France,—I cannot tell wat is baiser
en Anglish.   284

K. Hen. To kiss.

Alice. Your majesty entendre bettre que moi.

K. Hen. It is not a fashion for the maids in
France to kiss before they are married, would
she say?   289

Alice. Oui, vraiment.

K. Hen. O Kate! nice customs curtsy to great
kings. Dear Kate, you and I cannot be confined
within the weak list of a country's fashion: we 293
are the makers of manners, Kate; and the
liberty that follows our places stops the mouths
of all find-faults, as I will do yours, for uphold-
ing the nice fashion of your country in denying
me a kiss: therefore, patiently, and yielding 298
[*Kissing her*]. You have witchcraft in your lips,

291 curtsy: *bow*   293 list: *barrier*

Kate: there is more eloquence in a sugar touch
of them, than in the tongues of the French
council; and they should sooner persuade
Harry of England than a general petition of
monarchs. Here comes your father.   304

Enter the French Power, and the English Lords.

Bur. God save your majesty! My royal
cousin, teach you our princess English?

K. Hen. I would have her learn, my fair
cousin, how perfectly I love her; and that is
good English.   309

Bur. Is she not apt?

K. Hen. Our tongue is rough, coz, and my
condition is not smooth; so that, having neither
the voice nor the heart of flattery about me, I
cannot so conjure up the spirit of love in her,
that he will appear in his true likeness.   315

Bur. Pardon the frankness of my mirth if I
answer you for that. If you would conjure in
her, you must make a circle; if conjure up Love
in her in his true likeness, he must appear
naked and blind. Can you blame her then, 320
being a maid yet rosed over with the virgin
crimson of modesty, if she deny the appearance
of a naked blind boy in her naked seeing self?
It were, my lord, a hard condition for a maid
to consign to.   325

K. Hen. Yet they do wink and yield, as love
is blind and enforces.

Bur. They are then excused, my lord, when
they see not what they do.   329

318 circle; *cf. n.*

K. Hen. Then, good my lord, teach your cousin to consent winking.

Bur. I will wink on her to consent, my lord, if you will teach her to know my meaning: for maids, well summered and warm kept, are like flies at Bartholomew-tide, blind, though they 335 have their eyes; and then they will endure handling, which before would not abide looking on.

K. Hen. This moral ties me over to time and a hot summer; and so I shall catch the fly, your cousin, in the latter end, and she must be blind too. 341

Bur. As love is, my lord, before it loves.

K. Hen. It is so: and you may, some of you, thank love for my blindness, who cannot see many a fair French city for one fair French maid that stands in my way. 346

Fr. King. Yes, my lord, you see them perspectively, the cities turned into a maid; for they are all girdled with maiden walls that war hath never entered.

K. Hen. Shall Kate be my wife?

Fr. King. So please you. 352

K. Hen. I am content; so the maiden cities you talk of may wait on her: so the maid that stood in the way for my wish shall show me the way to my will. 356

Fr. King. We have consented to all terms of reason.

K. Hen. Is 't so, my lords of England?

West. The king hath granted every article: His daughter first, and then in sequel all, 361 According to their firm proposed natures.

335 Bartholomew-tide: *St. Bartholomew's day, August 24*
347 perspectively; *cf. n.*

Exe. Only he hath not yet subscribed this:
Where your majesty demands, that the King of
France, having any occasion to write for matter
of grant, shall name your highness in this form, 366
and with this addition, in French. Notre très cher
fils Henry roi d'Angleterre, Héritier de France;
and thus in Latin, Præclarissimus filius noster
Henricus, Rex Angliæ, et Hæres Franciæ.

Fr. King. Nor this I have not, brother, so denied,
But your request shall make me let it pass.   372

K. Hen. I pray you then, in love and dear alliance,
Let that one article rank with the rest;
And thereupon give me your daughter.

Fr. King. Take her, fair son; and from her blood
                    raise up   376
Issue to me; that the contending kingdoms
Of France and England, whose very shores look pale
With envy of each other's happiness,
May cease their hatred, and this dear conjunction
Plant neighbourhood and Christian-like accord
In their sweet bosoms, that never war advance
His bleeding sword 'twixt England and fair France.

All. Amen!   384

K. Hen. Now, welcome, Kate: and bear me witness
            all,
That here I kiss her as my sovereign queen.

                                              Flourish.

Q. Isa. God, the best maker of all marriages,
Combine your hearts in one, your realms in one!
As man and wife, being two, are one in love,   389
So be there 'twixt your kingdoms such a spousal
That never may ill office, or fell jealousy,
Which troubles oft the bed of blessed marriage,

363 subscribed: *signed*   367 addition: *title*
369 Præclarissimus; *cf. n.*   381 neighbourhood: *neighborly feeling*

Thrust in between the paction of these kingdoms,
To make divorce of their incorporate league;
That English may as French, French Englishmen,
Receive each other! God speak this Amen! 396
   All. Amen!
   K. Hen. Prepare we for our marriage: on which
     day,
My Lord of Burgundy, we'll take your oath,
And all the peers', for surety of our leagues. 400
Then shall I swear to Kate, and you to me;
And may our oaths well kept and prosperous be!
Sennet.   Exeunt.

EPILOGUE

Enter Chorus.

Thus far, with rough and all-unable pen,
   Our bending author hath pursu'd the story;
In little room confining mighty men, 3
   Mangling by starts the full course of their glory.
Small time, but in that small most greatly liv'd
   This star of England: Fortune made his sword,
By which the world's best garden he achiev'd, 7
   And of it left his son imperial lord.
Henry the Sixth, in infant bands crown'd King
   Of France and England, did this king succeed;
Whose state so many had the managing, 11
   That they lost France and made his England bleed:
Which oft our stage hath shown; and, for their sake,
In your fair minds let this acceptance take. 14

393 paction: *alliance*   402 S. d. Sennet: *set of notes on a trumpet*
2 bending: *i.e., bending beneath the burden of his task*
4 starts: *a fragmentary representation*   14 this: *this play*

FINIS.

NOTES

Prol. 11. *cockpit*. A pit or enclosure for the popular Elizabethan sport of cockfighting. The expression is not to be taken literally, but merely as part of Shakespeare's disparagement of his inadequate representation of the great events of King Henry's reign. The 'wooden O' of line 13 presumably refers to the Globe theatre, built in 1599. The Globe is thought to have been octagonal on the exterior, but the interior was probably circular.

Prol. 16. *Attest*. The 'crooked figure' that may stand for a million is probably the figure '1,' which was a very crooked figure as the Elizabethans wrote it.

Prol. 29. *jumping o'er times*. The action of the play covers a period of six years, from 1414 to 1420.

Prol. 32. *Chorus*. This term, an inheritance from the drama of Greece and Rome, is used by Shakespeare simply as a name by which to designate the speaker of his prologues; i.e., a single actor.

I. i. S. d. *Bishops*. The stage directions of the Folio do not discriminate between the titles of Archbishop and Bishop either here or in the second scene.

I. i. 35. *Hydra-headed*. The Hydra of Lerna was a nine-headed monster slain by Hercules. When one head was struck off, two new ones grew in its place.

I. i. 46. *Gordian knot*. An oracle had declared that he who untied this famous knot, tied by King Gordius of Phrygia, should rule over Asia. Alexander the Great cut the knot with his sword, declaring that he was destined to fulfill the oracle.

I. i. 51. *art*. The word as used here means the application of theory to practice. King Henry, reversing the usual process, appears to have learned the theory of statesmanship from practical endeavor

This, the Archbishop says, is strange, in view of the frivolity of his earlier years.

I. i. 89. *Edward.* King Henry's claim to the French throne rested upon his descent from Philip IV of France. Henry's great-grandfather, Edward III of England, was the son of Isabella, daughter to Philip IV. Her three brothers died without male heirs. Upon the death of the third (Charles IV), Isabella claimed the French throne for her son Edward; but an assembly of French peers and barons barred the English king's claim, declaring that 'no woman, nor therefore her son, could in accordance with custom succeed to the monarchy of France.' Later the doctrine thus enunciated became known as the Salic law. (Cf. I. ii. 38.) The crown of France passed to a younger branch of the French royal family of Capet.

I. ii. 11. *law Salique.* The Salic law is stated, in Latin, in line 38 below. (See preceding note.)

I. ii. 57. *four hundred one-and-twenty years.* In giving this figure, Shakespeare has perpetuated a mistake in arithmetic made by Holinshed. Throughout this long historical lecture Shakespeare is following his source very closely.

I. ii. 65. *King Pepin.* Pepin the Short, who usurped the throne of Childeric III in 751, was the first of the Carolingian family to take the title of King of the Franks.

I. ii. 69. *Hugh Capet.* First king of the family of Capet, who came to the throne in 987. The 'Lady Lingare' of line 74 appears to have been a totally fictitious personage. Ritson, commenting on this passage, says that 'these fictitious persons and pedigrees seem to have been devised by the English heralds.'

I. ii. 77. *Lewis the Tenth.* It should be Lewis the Ninth (Saint Louis, 1214-1270). Shakespeare copies the error from Holinshed.

I. ii. 94. *Than amply to imbar their crooked titles.*

This line has been variously interpreted according to the meaning attached to the word 'imbar.' It appears most reasonable to translate the word as 'to bar in' or 'to secure': The kings of France prefer to involve themselves in contradictions ('hide them in a net') rather than fully to secure their own titles by showing that although they are descended from the female, like King Henry, their claim is stronger than his.

I. ii. 106-114. The Archbishop is alluding to the battle of Crécy, August 26, 1346.

I. ii. 120. *May-morn of his youth.* King Henry was twenty-six years old.

I. ii. 126. *So hath your highness.* 'Your highness hath indeed what they think and know you have.' (Malone.) The emphasis is upon *hath.*

I. ii. 160. *impounded.* David Bruce, king of Scotland, was taken prisoner by the English at Nevill's Cross, October 17, 1346.

I. ii. 266. *chaces.* The word is a technical expression from the old game of tennis, used of the second impact on the floor of a ball which the opponent had failed or declined to return. The value of the chace was determined by the nearness of the spot of impact to the end wall. If the opponent, on changing sides, could better the stroke by causing his ball to rebound nearer the wall, he scored the point; otherwise it was scored by the first player. Hence the word *chaces* came to be practically equivalent to 'points scored,' and Harry seems to use it figuratively in that sense in this passage.

I. ii. 270. *living hence.* On account of his 'addiction to courses vain' in his younger days, Henry lost his place at the royal council-table and became 'almost an alien to the hearts of all the court.' (Cf. *Henry IV, Part 1*, III. ii. 32 ff.) In that sense he might be said to have been living in exile from his native royalty.

II. Chor. 31, 32. *Linger your patience on, etc.*
'Extend your patience, and we will overcome the ordinary limitations of distance and produce a play by pressing widely separated events into a narrow compass.'

II. Chor. 41, 42. *But, till . . . scene.* The meaning is quite obvious here, in spite of the curiously perverted construction: 'We shall shift our scene to Southampton; but not until the king comes forth.'

II. i. 6. *there shall be smiles.* Probably Nym means that when the time is ripe, the quarrel shall end in good humor.

II. i. 11. *there's an end.* Nym's language is a patchwork of the current phrases of the day, which he uses without any particular regard to their relevancy: 'that's the certain of it,' 'that is my rest,' 'things must be as they may,' 'there must be conclusions,' etc.

II. i. 17. *rest.* A technical term in the old game of *Primero,* meaning 'stake' or 'wager.'

II. i. 18. *that is the rendezvous of it.* This is but one more of Nym's current phrases, and it is not necessary to suppose that it carries any more meaning than the others.

II. i. 44. *Iceland dog.* Obviously Pistol means this to be a very scathing term of abuse. There are frequent references, in early seventeenth-century books, to the shaggy, snappish dogs brought over from Iceland to serve as lap-dogs. Whether Pistol had in mind their unhandsome appearance or their evil temper is uncertain.

II. i. 57. *Barbason.* Nym, unimpressed by the sound and fury of Pistol's speech, assures him that he cannot dispose of him, as conjurers dealt with fiends, by uttering high-sounding words.

II. i. 77. *hound of Crete.* Although some editors believe that Pistol means to imply that Nym is as bloodthirsty as a Cretan bloodhound, such an implication seems far-fetched and out of place here. Like the 'Iceland dog' of line 44, the expression is merely a term of abuse without any precise application, and chosen for no particular reason, unless it be Pistol's artistic craving for variety.

II. i. 79. *powdering-tub*. Literally, a tub in which meat was salted. Here it is used to denote the hot bath which formed part of the treatment for certain diseases.

II. i. 80. *kite of Cressid's kind*. This expression appears to have been a stock phrase in the literature of the day. Both Gascoigne and Greene use it. Henryson's *Testament of Cresseid* had told of Cressid's transformation into a leperous beggar (*lazar*).

II. i. 86. *thy face*. Bardolph's fiery complexion is the subject of more than one jest in *Henry IV*. Fluellen supplies us with further information on the same subject in III. vi. 110 ff.

II. i. 124. *quotidian tertian*. Dame Pistol has been so pleased with the learned sound of these medical terms that she uses them without any knowledge of their meaning. As a result, she confuses the quotidian fever, in which the paroxysms recur daily, with the tertian, in which the interval of recurrence is three days.

II. i. 130. *corroborate*. Of course the literal meaning of this word is quite inappropriate here; but that need not trouble us, as it obviously did not trouble Pistol, who uses it merely because it is a big word.

II. i. 133. *careers*. A term used to designate galloping a horse at full speed, backward and forward. Probably 'passes some careers' is Nym's way of saying 'Gives a free rein to his whims.'

II. ii. 118. *bade thee stand up*. 'Commanded thee to rise and do his bidding,' as one might give orders to a servant who could be relied upon for unquestioning obedience. Possibly, like the word *dub* in line 120, this is an allusion to the formula used in conferring knighthood.

II. ii. 155-157. *For me . . . intended.* 'Diuerse write that Richard earle of Cambridge did not conspire with the lord Scroope and Thomas Graie for the murthering of king Henrie to please the French king withall, but onelie to the intent to exalt to the crowne his brother in law Edmund earle of March as heire to Lionell duke of Clarence: after the death of which earle of March . . . the earl of Cambridge was sure that the crowne should come to him by his wife, and to his children, of hir begotten.' (Holinshed.)

II. iii. 9. *Arthur's bosom.* Obviously the hostess means Abraham's bosom. Cf. St. Luke 16. 22.

II. iii. 17, 18. *and a' babbled of green fields.* This is the famous emendation offered by Theobald (1688-1744) for the incomprehensible 'and a Table of greene fields' of the Folio.

II. iv. S. d. *Constable.* The Constable of France, originally the principal officer of the household of the French kings, was at this time the commander-in-chief of the French army in the absence of the monarch.

II. iv. 25. *Whitsun morris-dance.* Whitsuntide is the week commencing with Whitsunday (the seventh Sunday after Easter), especially the first three days of the week. The morris-dance was a fantastic dance which commonly formed part of the Whitsuntide festivities in English villages. The name 'morris' is derived from 'Moorish' and would seem to indicate that the dance was imported from Spain.

II. iv. 37. *Brutus.* The reference is to Lucius Junius Brutus, who simulated madness to conceal his plans for the liberation of his country from the tyranny of Tarquinius Superbus.

II. iv. 50. *flesh'd.* Hounds and hawks, in training for the chase, were fed with flesh.

III. ii. 3. *corporal.* In Act II, Scene i, Bardolph is called 'Lieutenant.'

III. ii. 6. *plain-song.* A simple melody without variations.

III. ii. 65. *the mines is not.* It is hardly necessary to point out the many irregularities in Captain Fluellen's use of singulars and plurals. He takes similar liberties with actives and passives and with the verbs 'to be' and 'to have.' In his speeches, as in those of the Scotch and Irish officers, dialect peculiarities are not explained unless they present unusual difficulties.

III. ii. 136-139. *Of my . . . nation.* Macmorris, who is of an excitable Celtic temperament, is quick to resent a fancied sneer at his country.

III. v. 7. *scions.* This word originally denoted small twigs cut from one tree and grafted upon another. The Dauphin is referring, of course, to the Norman extraction of the English.

III. v. 12. *but.* Grammatically the oath, 'Mort de ma vie,' governs this word. 'If these Englishmen march along uncontested, death take me if I do not sell my dukedom.'

III. v. 36. *Montjoy.* Not a name, but a title, borne by the chief heralds of France through many centuries. It is probable, however, that Shakespeare himself supposed that it was a name. Cf. III. vi. 150.

III. vi. S. d. *English and Welch.* The use of these words as synonyms for the names of Gower and Fluellen emphasizes Shakespeare's intention of representing national types in these captains.

III. vi. 13. *aunchient lieutenant.* Fluellen, with characteristic redundancy, gives Pistol two different titles.

III. vi. 42. *pax.* Perhaps this is a mistake for 'pyx,' the box containing the Host or consecrated wafer of the Mass. To steal a pyx would be a very serious sacrilege, and we know that on this expedition King Henry ordered a man hanged for such a theft. The pax, on the other hand, was a less sacred object—

the piece of wood or metal, engraved with the picture of Christ, which was given to the laity to be kissed during the celebration of the Mass.

III. vi. 62.   *The fig of Spain.*   Pistol merely repeats and elaborates the exclamation of line 59. 'Figo' was the Spanish word for 'fig.'

III. vii. 14.   *as if his entrails were hairs.*   The tennis balls of the day were stuffed with hair.   Cf. *Much Ado About Nothing,* III. ii. 46, 47.

III. vii. 19.   *pipe of Hermes.*   Hermes, by playing on his pipe, charmed the hundred-eyed Argus to sleep.

III. vii. 71, 72.   'The dog is turned to his own vomit again; and the sow that was washed to her wallowing in the mire.'   (2 Peter 2. 22.)

III. vii. 98.   *go to hazard.*   Shakespeare adopts this incident from Holinshed.   'The Frenchmen in the meanewhile, as though they had beene sure of victorie, made great triumphe, for the capteins had determined before how to diuide the spoile, and the soldiers the night before had plaid the Englishmen at dice.'

III. vii. 126.   *'tis a hooded valour.*   This is a metaphor drawn from falconry.   The hawk was kept hooded till it was released to fly at the game.   'To bate' was to flap the wings, as the hawk invariably did, after being unhooded, preparatory to flight. Probably the Constable uses this word punningly with a play upon another meaning of 'bate': to dwindle, to diminish.

IV. i. 55.   *Saint Davy's day.*   It was an old Welsh custom to wear a leek upon Saint David's day to commemorate the victory said to have been won by King Arthur over the Saxons on Saint David's day in the year 540 A. D.   It is the tradition that the battle was fought in a garden where leeks were growing and that Saint David ordered Arthur's soldiers to wear the leek in honour of the victory.   Shakespeare refers to this custom in two other passages in this play: IV. vi. 102 ff. and V. i. 74.

IV. i. 246. *French crowns.* There is a double pun here: a play upon two different meanings of 'crown,' and an allusion to the crime of clipping gold coins.

IV. i. 283. *The farced title.* Perhaps there is an allusion here to the herald that goes before the king and proclaims his full title in high-sounding phrases. More probably *running 'fore* means 'prefixed to' the name of the king.

IV. i. 321. *chantries.* Originally a chantry was an endowment for the maintenance of one or more priests to sing daily mass for the souls of the founders or others specified by them. Later it came to mean a chapel, altar, or part of a church so endowed.

IV. i. 323-325. *Though all that I can do, etc.* King Henry acknowledges that such works of piety as the founding of chantries have availed him nothing; not by such means can he cleanse his conscience of the sense of guilt. After all that he can do, he must still penitently implore pardon.

IV. ii. 36. *dare the field.* Another phrase borrowed from the terminology of falconry. The bird was said to be 'dared' when it was so terrified by the hawk that it kept close to the ground.

IV. ii. 60, 61. The French 'thought themselues so sure of victorie, that diuerse of the noble men made such hast towards the battell, that they left manie of their seruants and men of warre behind them, and some of them would not once staie for their standards: as, amongst other, the duke of Brabant, when his standard was not come, caused a baner to be taken from a trumpet and fastened to a speare; the which he commanded to be borne before him in steed of his standard.' (Holinshed.)

IV. iii. 57. *Crispin Crispian.* Saint Crispin's day was sacred to two brothers, Crispinus and Crispianus,

who were martyred for their faith at Soissons early
in the fourth century.

IV. iv. S. d. *Excursions*. This stage direction indicates that small groups of armed men hurry across
the stage as if in the heat of battle.

IV. iv. 4. *Qualtitie calmie custure me*. This is the
reading of the Folio. The passage is usually emended
to read, 'Quality? Calen O custure me!' The last
four words in this amended reading form the refrain
of a popular Irish song of Shakespeare's day and are
a corruption of the Irish phrase, 'Colleen, oge asture,'
i.e., 'young girl, my treasure.' According to this conjecture, Pistol repeats the only word he has under-
stood in the French gentleman's speech and follows
it by quoting, with characteristic irrelevancy, the
burden of this popular song. The present editor has
restored the Folio reading because the resemblance
between Pistol's words and the burden of the song
is not close enough to be altogether convincing; but
the theory represents the most satisfactory explana-
tion that has been offered. C. D. Stewart (*Some
Textual Difficulties in Shakespeare*, Yale University
Press, 1914, pp. 71-74) argues that Pistol is trying to
talk French: 'Quel titre comme accoster me.'

IV. iv. 14. *moys*. Probably the French 'muys' or
'muids,' a measure of corn, equal to five quarters English measure. It has also been suggested that 'moys'
were some sort of coin.

IV. iv. 76. *devil i' the old play*. This refers not
to any particular play, but to the old Morality plays,
in which the Devil was frequently the butt of the
Vice or clown, who, armed with a wooden dagger, sub-
jected him to all manner of physical indignities. The
'roaring devil' in these plays presented just such a
combination of braggadocio and cowardice as Pistol.

IV. vii. 104. *in a garden*. This is another reference to the traditional Arthurian battle in the leek-
garden. Cf. IV. i. 55 and note.

IV. vii. 105. *Monmouth caps.* These caps were soft and flat, with a plume, and were worn particularly by soldiers. As their name indicates, they were originally made at Monmouth, where the cap-making industry appears to have flourished. 'The best caps were formerly made at Monmouth, where the Capper's Chapel doth still remain.' (Fuller, *Worthies of Wales,* 1660.)

IV. viii. 128. *Non nobis.* This is the one hundred and fifteenth psalm, which begins, in the Latin version, 'Non nobis, Domine, non nobis, sed nomini tuo da gloriam.'

V. Chor. 30. *general.* Robert Devereux, Earl of Essex, set out from London on March 27, 1599, to suppress Tyrone's rebellion in Ireland. (Cf. Appendix B.) His return was by no means the triumph which Shakespeare prophesies in these lines. He mismanaged his campaign most conspicuously, frequently acting in opposition to the commands of the queen, and finally concluded a truce with Tyrone in September in order that he might be free to return to London and vindicate himself before the queen. In the following June he was called before a special court to answer for his mismanagement of the mission and was deprived of his offices.

V. Chor. 38. *emperor's.* In five lines the Chorus passes over the events of four years. Emperor Sigismund landed at Dover on May 1, 1416, about six months after the battle of Agincourt, and immediately set about his task of making peace between England and France; but it was not until May, 1420, that the peace treaty was signed. Shakespeare makes no reference to Henry's second military expedition to France and the long siege of Rouen.

V. ii. 17. *basilisks.* The basilisk cannon was named after a fabulous serpent, the basilisk or cockatrice, that was said to kill its victims with a glance.

V. ii. 138. *measure.* Shakespeare frequently plays on the various meanings of this word. Here he first uses the word in the sense of 'metre'; secondly, of 'dancing'; and thirdly, of 'amount.'

V. ii. 155. *let thine eye be thy cook.* Let thine eye dress me in attractions to suit thy taste.

V. ii. 160. *uncoined constancy.* Henry means that his love has not been stamped out into the form of glib phrases such as pass current among more accomplished but less sincere lovers.

V. ii. 262. *broken music.* 'Part music,' arranged for different kinds of instruments.

V. ii. 318. *circle.* The making of a circle was part of the elaborate preparations of conjurers for the exercise of their magic. Within the circle the conjurer was supposed to be immune from the baleful influences of the evil spirits that he raised.

V. ii. 347. *perspectively.* As through a 'perspective,' i.e., an instrument producing fantastic optical illusions.

V. ii. 369. *Præclarissimus.* Once more Shakespeare has copied one of Holinshed's errors. The word should be 'præcarissimus,' the Latin equivalent for the French 'très cher.'

APPENDIX A

Sources of the Play

Virtually all the historical material for *Henry V* was drawn from Raphael Holinshed's *Chronicles of England, Scotland, and Ireland* (Second Edition, 1587). A few minor incidents—the embassy of the tennis balls, Pistol's encounter with the French soldier, and the wooing scene of Act V—seem to have been suggested by the crude old chronicle play, *The Famous Victories of Henry V*, licensed for the press in 1594. The characters of the sub-plot—Pistol, Fluellen, and the rest—are entirely original.

Shakespeare follows Holinshed almost word for word in certain passages of the play; particularly in the account of the bill against the clergy, in the Archbishop's argument in favor of Henry's claim to the French throne, and in the list of the casualties at the battle of Agincourt. More typical of his usual treatment of his sources are the passages in which he has caught up a suggestion or two from the prosy chronicle and transformed them into glowing poetry. The following quotation from Holinshed, for example, contains the only hints which Shakespeare found in his source for King Henry's stirring appeal to his officers on the morning of Saint Crispin's day:

'It is said, that as he heard one of the host vtter his wish to another thus: I would to God there were with vs now so manie good soldiers as are at this houre within England! the king answered: I would not wish a man more here than I haue; we are indeed in comparison to the enimies but a few, but if God of his clemencie doo fauour vs, and our iust cause, (as I trust he will,) we shall speed well inough. But let no man ascribe victorie to our owne strength and

might, but onelie to God's assistance; to whome I
haue no doubt we shall worthilie haue cause to giue
thanks therefore. And if so be that for our offenses
sakes we shall be deliuered into the hands of our
enimies, the lesse number we be, the lesse damage
shall the realme of England susteine; but if we should
fight in trust of multitude of men, and so get the
victorie, (our minds being prone to pride,) we should
therevpon peraduenture ascribe the victorie not so
much to the gift of God, as to our owne puissance,
and thereby prouoke his high indignation and displeasure against vs: and if the enimie get the vpper
hand, then should our realme and countrie suffer
more damage and stand in further danger. But be
you of good comfort, and shew your selues valiant!
God and our iust quarrell shall defend vs, and deliuer
these our proud aduersaries with all the multitude of
them which you see (or at the least the most of them)
into our hands.'

APPENDIX B

The History of the Play

The production of *Henry V* has been assigned, on
very substantial evidence, to the year 1599. Francis
Meres, giving a list of Shakespeare's plays in a book
published in 1598, makes no mention of *Henry V,*
although his list includes *Henry IV*. The play was
entered on the Stationers' Register in August, 1600,
and the first edition was published in that year. The
reference to the 'wooden O' in line 13 of the Prologue
is usually supposed to be an allusion to the Globe
Theatre, which was completed in 1599. Most sig-
nificant of all, the lines in the Prologue to Act V
referring to the Earl of Essex must have been written

and spoken during the earl's absence in Ireland, which extended from March 27 until September 28, 1599.

Three very imperfect editions of the play appeared prior to the publication of the First Folio in 1623. The First Quarto (1600) omits all the prologues, the epilogue, and several entire scenes. These and other omissions, notably in the long speeches, which are much curtailed, shorten the play by some seventeen hundred lines. The errors and absurdities of the edition are many; particularly in the scenes written in French (which is very 'fausse French' indeed as it appears in this volume), and in the prose scenes, where an heroic attempt has been made to transform the prose into poetry. It is now generally believed that the First Quarto is an imperfect edition of a shortened acting version of the play, and it may have been made up for the press largely from notes taken in the theatre during a performance. The Second Quarto (1602) and the Third Quarto, dated 1608, but really printed in 1619, are reprints of the edition of 1600, very slightly amended and without independent value. Modern editors accept the text of the First Folio (1623) as the most reliable, and have adopted the reading of the Quartos in only a few instances.

A funeral elegy on Richard Burbage, Shakespeare's most famous fellow actor, gives us the information that the part of King Henry was one in which Burbage won distinction. The unknown writer laments:

> Poor Romeo never more shall tears beget
> For Juliet's love and cruel Capulet;
> Harry shall not be seen as king or prince,
> They died with thee, dear Dick (and not long since.)

This is the only bit of information we have as to the early stage history of *Henry V*. The records of Sir Henry Herbert show that a play entitled 'Henry the 5th' was licensed for the stage in 1663, but it is not certain that this record refers to Shakespeare's play. We have positive record of a performance given at Covent Garden Theatre, February 23, 1738. Seven years later, at the time of the last Jacobite rising, the play was once more presented at the same theatre, perhaps by way of stirring the patriotism of the Londoners at a time when the Scots were marching on the city and France was supposed to be preparing to invade England. In this latter performance, the part of Pistol was played by the younger Cibber. Garrick presented the play at Drury Lane on December 16, 1747, but left the part of King Henry to Barry, appearing himself as the Chorus, in the costume of the day—'a full-dress court suit with powdered bag-wig, ruffles, and sword.'

Under the lavish management of Rich, Covent Garden gave a very elaborate production in 1761, including an interpolated scene, borrowed from *Henry IV, Part 2,* representing the coronation procession. The popular actress, George Anne Bellamy, walked in the procession as Queen. Another spectacular touch was added in the revival of 1769 at the same theatre by the introduction of the Champion (of the coronation ceremony) in full armor and on horseback. Drury Lane revived the play for the first time in twenty years in 1789, with John Philip Kemble as Henry; and the same actor performed the part from time to time during his career. He secured a telling stage effect at the close of Act IV by suddenly interrupting his prayer, at the sound of the trumpet, and rushing off the stage sword in hand. On March 8, 1830, Edmund Kean appeared at Drury Lane in the rôle of King Henry. His memory failed him during the performance and he was obliged to apologize to the audience from the stage. During the nineteenth century the play was performed also by William Macready, Samuel Phelps and Charles Kean. The production given by the latter at the Princess's

Theatre in 1859 was a very ambitious undertaking and met with so great a success that the play ran to eighty-four performances. Kean attached a great deal of importance to historical accuracy. His setting for the siege of Harfleur was constructed after careful study of a Latin manuscript giving an account of the siege as seen by a priest who accompanied the army. A further spectacular effect was secured by transforming the description of Henry's return to London, as given by the Chorus, into an actual stage spectacle. Mrs. Charles Kean recited the prologues in the character of Clio, Muse of History. The most conspicuous production in England during the twentieth century was given by Lewis Waller at the Lyceum Theatre in 1900, at the time when the Boer war had stimulated British patriotism. Lily Hanbury appeared as Chorus in Waller's production.

In America, the first performance of the play of which we have any record took place at the Park Theatre in New York in 1804, with Cooper as King Henry. Macready and Waller brought their productions to this country from England, the latter in 1912. In 1876 John Coleman produced the play in New York at great expense, but it ran for only a week. Most noteworthy of the American performances is Richard Mansfield's magnificent presentation in 1900. The production opened at the Garden Theatre, New York City, October 3, after the most elaborate preparations, and had a very successful run, playing to crowded houses in New York, Philadelphia, and Chicago. Mansfield stated that he was led to produce the play by 'a consideration of its healthy and virile tone, so diametrically in contrast to many of the performances now current.'

A great memorial performance of *Henry V* in London, May 4, 1916, attracted a 'full and enthusiastic' house, and evoked comments upon the contemporaneous effect of many scenes.

APPENDIX C

By permission of the Oxford University Press, the
text of this edition of *Henry V* is that of Craig's
Oxford Shakespeare, with the following alterations:

1. The stage directions are those of the First Folio,
with necessary additions indicated by brackets.

2. French passages throughout the play have in
general been modernized.

3. A few changes have been made in punctuation
(such as *what, man* for *what man* in II. iii. 19); and
the spelling of the following words has been nor-
malized: warlike, ooze, ordnance, antics, villainy,
wrecked, lackey, embattl'd.

4. All other departures from Craig's text repre-
sent reversions to the reading of the First Folio. In
the following list of such changes, the reading of the
present edition stands first in the line: the reading of
the Oxford Shakespeare follows the colon.

I. ii. 22	our: the
I. ii. 30	For: And
I. ii. 74	th' heir: heir
I. ii. 99	man: son
I. ii. 151	assays: essays
I. ii. 208	Come: Fly
II. Chor. 31	on, and we'll: on; and well
II. Chor. 32	distance; force: distance while we force
II. i. 75	Couple a gorge: Coupe le gorge
II. ii. 104	and: from
II. ii. 179, 180	give You patience: give you Patience
II. iv. 1	comes: come
II. iv. 57	mountain sire: mounting sire
II. iv. 75, 115	brother of: brother
III. i. 34	Harry, England, and: Harry! England and
III. ii. 50, 51	fire-shovel: I knew . . . coals. They: fire-shovel;—I knew . . . coals—they

III. ii. 69	yard: yards
III. ii. 79	beard: peard
III. ii. 120	call: calls
III. ii. 129	pay 't: pay it
III. ii. 145, 157	war: wars
III. v. 41	of Berri: Berri
III. vii. 15	chez: qui a
III. vii. 54	Nay, for: Ma foi,
IV. Chor. 28	O now: O! now
IV. Chor. 45	fear, that mean and gentle all: fear.— Then mean and gentle all,
IV. i. 35	Che vous la: Qui va là
IV. i. 47	from heart-string: from my heart-string
IV. i. 77	hear: heard
IV. i. 154	who: whom
IV. i. 260	idol: idle
IV. i. 312	Lord,: Lord!
IV. ii. 49	gimmal'd: gimmal
IV. iv. 4	Qualtitie calmie custure me: Quality? Calen O custure me!
IV. iv. 39	Owy: Ouy
IV. vi. 15	He cries aloud, 'Tarry, my: And cries aloud, 'Tarry, dear
IV. vii. 7	ha': have
IV. vii. 167	and: an
IV. viii. 10	world: 'orld
IV. viii. 37, 38	and will avouchment: and avouchments
IV. viii. 100	Great Master … Guichard … Dolphin: Great-master … Guischard … Dauphin
IV. viii. 101	Anthony: Antony
IV. viii. 130	And then: We'll then
V. i. 7	world: 'orld
V. i. 39	leek, you: leek you
V. i. 86	Doll: Nell
V. i. 90	cudgell'd: cudgelled
V. ii. 40	it: its
V. ii. 54	all: as
V. ii. 55	wildness.: wildness,
V. ii. 102	shall: sall
V. ii. 108	wat: vat
V. ii. 135	well: vell
V. ii. 186	wat: vat
V. ii. 266	shall: sall
V. ii. 269	shall: sall
V. ii. 283	wat: vat

APPENDIX D

INDEX OF WORDS GLOSSED

(Figures in full-faced type refer to page-numbers)

gage: 75 (IV. i. 226)
galled: 40 (III. i. 12)
galliard: 15 (I. ii. 252)
galling: 107 (V. i. 78)
garb: 107 (V. i. 81)
gentle his condition: 84 (IV. iii. 63)
gesture: 66 (IV. Chor. 25)
giddy: 11 (I. ii. 145)
gilt: 18 (II. Chor. 26)
gimmal'd: 81 (IV. ii. 49)
gipes: 93 (IV. vii. 53)
girded: 39 (III. Chor. 27)
gleeking: 107 (V. i. 78)
glistering: 28 (II. ii. 117)
gloze: 7 (I. ii. 40)
go about: 75 (IV. i. 215)
go to hazard: 63 (III. vii. 98)
God before: 16 (I. ii. 307)
God-den: 44 (III. ii. 93)
good sort: 101 (IV. viii. 80)
grace of kings: 18 (II. Chor. 28)
grandfather: 95 (IV. vii. 96)
grant: 103 (V. Chor. 7)
great sort: 96 (IV. vii. 143)
greener: 38 (II. iv. 136)
greenly: 113 (V. ii. 148)
groat: 106 (V. i. 62)
grossly: 27 (II. ii. 107)
gulf: 33 (II. iv. 10)
gull: 56 (III. vi. 72)
gun-stones: 16 (I. ii. 282)

habit: 57 (III. vi. 124)
had: 77 (IV. i. 300)
haggled: 91 (IV. vi. 11)
Hampton: 27 (II. ii. 91)
handle: 32 (II. iii. 39)
hard-favour'd: 40 (III. i. 8)
hazard: 15 (I. ii. 263)
head, in: 24 (II. ii. 18)
heady: 3 (I. i. 34); 47 (III. iii. 32)
hearts: 78 (IV. i. 312)

help Hyperion to his horse: 77 (IV. i. 295)
hilding: 80 (IV. ii. 29)
his: 3 (I. i. 36)
honour-owing: 91 (IV. vi. 9)
housewifery: 33 (II. iii. 66)
humorous: 34 (II. iv. 28)
huswife: 107 (V. i. 85)
Hydra-headed: 3 (I. i. 35)

imaginary: 1 (I. Chor. 18)
imagin'd wing: 38 (III. Chor. 1)
imp: 69 (IV. i. 45)
impawn: 7 (I. ii. 21)
impeachment: 59 (III. vi. 154)
impounded: 11 (I. ii. 160)
in few: 14 (I. ii. 245)
in fresher robes: 86 (IV. iii. 117)
in lieu of: 15 (I. ii. 255)
indirectly: 36 (II. iv. 94)
instance: 23 (II. ii. 119)
intelligence: 17 (II. Chor. 12)
intendment: 11 (I. ii. 144)
intertissued: 77 (IV. i. 282)
investing: 66 (IV. Chor. 26)
irreconciled: 73 (IV. i. 162)
is come after: 93 (IV. vii. 34, 35)
is pear: 99 (IV. viii. 37)
issue: 91 (IV. vi. 34)
it: 109 (V. ii. 40)

jack-an-apes: 113 (V. ii. 147)
Jack-sauce: 97 (IV. vii. 149)
jades: 51 (III. v. 19)
jealousy: 28 (II. ii. 126)
Jewry: 48 (III. iii. 40)
just notice: 96 (IV. vii. 123)
jutty: 40 (III. i. 13)

kecksies: 109 (V. ii. 52)
kern: 62 (III. vii. 59)

sa': **45** (III. ii. 122)
sack: **31** (II. iii. 29)
sad-ey'd: **13** (I. ii. 202)
Saint Davy's day: **69** (IV. i. 55)
Saint Denis: **114** (V. ii. 192)
Salique: **6** (I. ii. 11)
sand: **71** (IV. i. 101)
'Sblood: **93** (IV. viii. 9)
scaffold: **1** (I. Chor. 10)
scald: **104** (V. i. 5)
scambling (adj.): **2** (I. i. 4)
scambling (n.): **115** (V. ii. 217)
sconce: **56** (III. vi. 78)
seat: **15** (I. ii. 269)
second accent: **37** (II. iv. 126)
self: **2** (I. i. 1)
sennet: **121** (V. ii. 402 S. d.)
senses: **32** (II. iii. 52)
sequestration: **4** (I. i. 58)
set: **18** (II. Chor. 34)
severals: **5** (I. i. 86)
shales: **79** (IV. ii. 18)
shog: **20** (II. i. 47)
show: **28** (II. ii. 127)
shows: **71** (IV. i. 108)
shrewdly: **61** (III. vii. 55)
signal: **103** (V. Chor. 21)
signs: **30** (II. ii. 192)
sinister: **36** (II. iv. 85)
skirr: **94** (IV. vii. 65)
slips, in the: **41** (III. i. 31)
slovenry: **85** (IV. iii. 114)
snatchers: **11** (I. ii. 143)
sooth: **59** (III. vi. 154)
sort: **104** (V. Chor. 25)
sorts: **12** (I. ii. 190)
speculation: **80** (IV. ii. 31)
speed, be my: **114** (V. ii. 193)
spiritualty: **10** (I. ii. 132)
spital: **21** (II. i. 78)
sprays: **51** (III. v. 5)
Staines: **30** (II. iii. 2)

starts: **121** (Epil. 4)
sternage, to: **39** (III. Chor. 18)
still: **11** (I. ii. 145); **73** (IV. i. 322)
stilly: **66** (IV. Chor. 5)
stood on: **56** (III. vi. 80)
stoop: **71** (IV. i. 113)
straight: **30** (II. ii. 191)
straight strossers: **62** (III. vii. 60)
subscribed: **120** (V. ii. 363)
suddenly: **111** (V. ii. 81)
sufferance, by his: **25** (II. ii. 46)
sufferance, in: **29** (II. ii. 159)
suggest: **27** (II. ii. 114)
supply, for the which: **2** (I. Chor. 31)
sur-rein'd: **51** (III. v. 19)
sutler: **22** (II. i. 116)
swashers: **42** (III. ii. 31)
swill'd with: **40** (III. i. 14)
sympathize with: **65** (III. vii. 163)

take: **20** (II. i. 55)
tall: **21** (II. i. 72)
Tartar: **28** (II. ii. 123)
task: **6** (I. ii. 6)
Tavy's: **95** (IV. vii. 109)
temper: **113** (V. ii. 152)
temper'd: **28** (II. ii. 118)
tender: **30** (II. ii. 175)
tenours: **110** (V. ii. 72)
terms: **100** (IV. viii. 43)
that: **4** (I. i. 47)
them: **9** (I. ii. 93)
theoric: **4** (I. i. 52)
tike: **19** (II. i. 31)
to: **62** (III. vii. 65)
toward: **98** (IV. viii. 4)
troth-plight: **19** (II. i. 21)
Troyan: **105** (V. i. 20)
trumpet: **81** (IV. ii. 61)